The Living Proof

I Have Found the Fountain of Youth

by
Noel Johnson

BRITIC (USA), INC.

18 East 53rd Street • New York, NY 10022
7825 Fay Avenue • Ste. 200 • La Jolla, CA 92037
2nd Printing

Notice

It is not the purpose of this book to prescribe or treat. Such should be left to qualified practitioners. The purpose of this book is to chronicle the life of Noel Johnson and the related life style that has led to his physical rejuvenation.

While his program may be unique to himself, documented scientific information has been included when available and necessary. The authors and publishers of this book shall have neither liability nor responsibility to any person or entity with respect to any loss or damage caused or alleged to be caused directly or indirectly by the information contained in this book.

We are confident that you will find benefit from the use of this book and that if you are not satisfied for any reason, you may return it for a full refund.

Copyright © 1989 by BRITIC (USA), Inc.

All rights reserved, including the right to reproduce this book or portions thereof in any form, except for the inclusion of brief quotations in a review. The text of this book or any part thereof, may not be reproduced or transmitted in any form or by any means without the prior written permission of the author/publisher.

Library of Congress Catalog Card No. 89-60783
ISBN 0-9622287-0-2

Cover Design: MIKE STEIN

Book Production By **MIPRO PRINTING**
La Jolla, California 92037

Printed in the United States of America.

Acknowledgements

Several years ago I wrote my first book, *A Dud at 70, A Stud at 80*. Since that publication I have seen more corners of the world than I ever dreamed, I have lectured to medical professionals, I have learned from them in return, and I have proven in performance what was yet theory in the first book.

The Living Proof: I Have Found the Fountain of Youth is a new book, one that truly represents my story and my recommendations on how you can achieve and enjoy the very best of health and long, positive life.

For making this book possible I must recognize and commend my friend and business counsel, Ragnar Th. Breidfjord of Kristiansand, Norway, and his new Britic U.S.A. company. My son and daughter—Jim and Betty Lou—must be acknowledged first because of their vital concern for me when I was a dud, a physical failure, and then for their support, encouragement, and participation through my transformation and accomplishments.

I thank the thousands of writers, broadcasters, and interviewers in newspapers, magazines, radio, and television throughout the world who have carried my teaching in their own effective words, columns, and programs. I appreciate them, too, for the reportage they will do on this book and on its message of health and vitality.

I also commend you for buying this book and reading it, then for gaining from it your best of health and future.

Noel Johnson
San Diego, California
January 1989

About This Book

This book tells the story of one man's remarkable return to health and fitness as a role model for others. The story is true; the facts have been researched; the book is a living history and testament to the ability of the human body to restore itself if given proper nutrition, exercise, and attitude.

This book is not intended to offer medical advice, nor is it presented with any such warranty. Its concepts, though, have worked and are working for millions of people around the world who have witnessed and learned from Noel Johnson.

Table of Contents

Chapter One:
THE PROMISE — 1

Chapter Two:
THE NOEL JOHNSON OF YESTERDAY — 12

Chapter Three:
HOW I TURNED MY LIFE AROUND — 24

Chapter Four:
HOW TO CURE IMPOTENCE — 37

Chapter Five:
GET ON THE PATH — 47

Chapter Six:
EXERCISE—GET YOUR BODY MOVING — 60

Chapter Seven:
NUTRITION—HEALTH DEPENDS ON WHAT YOU EAT OR DO NOT EAT — 78

Chapter Eight:
HONEYBEE POLLEN—THE NUTRITIONAL MIRACLE — 92

Chapter Nine:
BREATHING RIGHT FOR HEALTH — 102

Chapter Ten:
YOUR MIND POWER IS THE KEY TO
UNLOCKING A HEALTHY LIFE   **115**

Chapter Eleven:
WHAT'S NEXT?   **132**

Chapter Twelve:
THE CARE-FOR-YOURSELF PROGRAM   **144**

Chapter Thirteen:
THE CHIROPRACTIC CONNECTION   **153**

Chapter Fourteen:
POLLEN IS A NECESSITY FOR LONGEVITY   **161**

In Conclusion:
A CHALLENGE   **166**

Chapter One

THE PROMISE

How old would you be if you didn't know how old you were?
—Leroy (Satchel) Paige

In 1970, at age 71, I had high blood pressure, arthritis, gout, and bursitis. I was 40 pounds over my normal weight of 135 and I could barely climb a flight of stairs without wheezing. My heart had been acting up with an uneven rhythm since 1966. Things were so bad, in fact, that in 1968, my life insurance company cancelled my coverage because I was such a risk. Finally, my doctor advised me that any physical activity could be extremely dangerous—even fatal. He warned, "If you even try to mow the lawn you may never get to trim the edges."

How did I get into such poor physical shape? After all, I saw myself as having lived a fairly normal life. Oh, I had had the usual childhood diseases and more than my share of colds, flu, and other ailments. Then, as an adult I had half a kidney removed and had undergone other operations as well.

I grew up, married, had children and worked hard so that my family and I could enjoy what Americans often call "the good life," complete with backyard barbecues with friends and neighbors, vacation trips, and the usual collection of material

1

possessions. My wife Zola and I had planned to travel during our retirement years, but when that time came I found my physical condition sliding downhill rapidly. It seemed that perhaps without even being aware of it, I had deteriorated into a sickly old man.

At least a couple of reasons were responsible for my decline. First and foremost were the decades of living what was then the average American life-style—including ample portions of rich food and almost no exercise. Then, in 1969, my beloved helpmate suffered a series of strokes that put her into a coma. For the next two years, I stayed at home most of the time, sitting in a daze, eating whatever was at hand, drinking beer and watching television. I was convinced then that the next step would be either a nursing home or "six feet under."

But one day I was jolted out of my apathy and I began considering the possibility that, "Maybe it's not too late to change things."

As it turned out, it wasn't.

TRANSFORMATION BEGINS

By early November 1971 —after two years of conditioning—articles began appearing in California newspapers describing a series of tests performed on me by Dr. Jack Wilmore, an exercise physiologist at the University of California, Davis. I was 71 at the time and I had been following a health-care program that I had created myself.

The *Sacramento Bee* headlined its article "Superman Is Studied at UCSD." It quoted me as saying that I had begun this serious training program because I was "darn stubborn and just don't want to get old."

The copy noted that I had won gold medals in three races (one mile, 10,000 meters, and 26.2 miles) and that I had been named the most outstanding athlete over 70 at the Amateur Athletic Union's Annual Masters Track and Field Meet.[1]

Another article, entitled "Youthful Vitality Fuels Superman," noted how I was running 50 miles a week and eating a dozen times a day, "but never much and seldom meat."

A *San Diego Union* article began by saying "Three years ago, Noel Johnson of San Diego had heart trouble and generally did not feel in top shape." (That was an understatement.) "Today he is 40 pounds lighter, runs the mile in 6 1/2 minutes and wins gold medals at track meets."

The *San Francisco Examiner* observed that "Exercise Makes a Superman," then went on to quote my comment that "most people consider me a darn fool, but almost every day people ask me what my doctor thinks about all this and how I reply that 'I don't seek his advice.'"

Dr. Wilmore put me through a gauntlet of tests that monitored my heart, measured my maximum oxygen intake, and tested my physical condition. He had me run for nine minutes on a treadmill that was slanted uphill for half of the time. Every 15 seconds his instruments measured my heartbeat, breathing rate, oxygen intake and other functions.

In response to the results, he said, "This man is a superman."

---

[1] Noel Johnson currently holds all records for long-distance running (more than six miles) in the 70-75 age category of the AAU Masters Program and as of this writing is the only one his age running marathons.

Dr. Wilmore was conducting a research project to define biological aging—as opposed to social aging. He explained that, to date, biological aging refers to the poorly understood natural changes that take place between birth and death, while social aging refers to the fact that some people become prematurely old because of poor diet and slack exercise habits.

I was happy to have the good doctor prove my point by saying that my improved physical condition over the past couple of years showed that, with proper activity and eating and drinking habits, humans can decrease their biological age.

In 1979, Dr. Lenore Zohman, a cardiologist at Montefiore Hospital in New York City, was quoted as saying that

> Noel looks like he's in his early 60s and has the legs of a man in his 30s. Noel is refuting the misconception that we must decline with age, that aging is degeneration. Diseases in older adults don't have to be accepted as part of the aging process. Heart disease is not necessarily concomitant to getting old. Noel's irregular [heart] rhythm would ordinarily be considered abnormal, but is not abnormal for him.

She noted that the average person my age—I was then 80—would reach exhaustion at 140 beats per minute. "Noel tested at 162. Quite remarkable."

In June 1981, after he had put me through a treadmill test, Exercise Physiologist Bill Phillips at San Diego State University, said, "We can't say he's reversing the aging process, but he's sure holding his own against it." Dr. Phillips, along with physiology professor Tony Sucec, likened my performance to that of an average man aged 30 to 39. During the initial run on the treadmill, my heart rate reached 162. My aerobic threshold, the point where fatigue sets in as the body reaches it maximum capacity to function with oxygen consumed, was that of a man half my age. Test results showed no significant decline since the tests run a decade earlier (1971), and again in 1979 at Montefiore Hospital in New York.

"These results show," said Dr. Phillips, "that at 80 a person can live a full and active life if a decision is made to change the life-style that contributes to degeneration. It's a matter of choosing to invest the time and effort earlier in life so that you can do the things you want to do later on." At the time, I weighed 147—about 5 to 10 pounds above normal for a 5'7" frame.

Remarkable? Perhaps. But maybe not because I do not think I am very different from most people. I believe health is a matter of attitude and intention.

As of today, I have completed more long-distance races than I can remember in England, Norway, Denmark, Iceland, Thailand, and Japan, as well as the United States. I have finished the prestigious New York Marathon six times, and my best time was 5 hours and 42 minutes.

I have run the 13.2 mile uphill portion of the Pikes Peak Marathon three times, the first when I was 73. It's said to be the most grueling race in the world—so tough that most 20 year olds don't finish. The rugged trail goes across streams and over fields, rocks, and fallen trees. In one area, the narrow path has a sheer cliff face on one side and a 500-foot drop-off on the other. At 12,000 feet, vegetation ceases to grow. The finish line is at an elevation of more than 14,000 feet, where there is about half the amount of oxygen we breathe at sea level. By the time I got to the top the first time, my heart was beating so fast I thought it was going to jump right out of my rib cage.

Three weeks after my sixth New York Marathon, on November 22, 1987, I was in Bangkok competing in Thailand's Royal Marathon in honor of King Phumiphon Adunyadet's 60th birthday. I remained in the Far East to participate in several boxing matches.

Today, I not only receive letters from all over the world with people asking how I managed to reverse the aging process, but I travel to many countries to lecture on the subject.

MUST WE BE SICK?

Many people in the medical profession still believe that as the years pass and as we reach middle age and beyond we automatically increase sickness and debility. As a guest on the Tom Snyder Show in Los Angeles a few years ago, I was paired with a geriatric specialist from Philadelphia. Heavyset and flushed, this doctor did not look healthy. He informed me that a month earlier he had suffered a severe heart attack. He paused, then added, "You know, it's normal for a person who reaches 65 or 70 to have such diseases."

I was then in my early 70s and so asked him, "Doc, I'm past that age, so why don't I have such ailments?"

He replied, "Well, you may be that one person in a million that we call a freak, but everybody else will have them."

I couldn't stop myself from saying, "Doctor, I wish that you would live long enough to find that I'm just like those other people but that I'm never going to have them."

So maybe I'm boasting, but I have been there. I had those ailments and more in 1970. The difference in my case is that I left that state of dismal health and heart troubles behind.

I am now more physically active than ever before. I run about 20 miles every week, bounce for an hour each day on a mini trampoline, and do arm lifts with light weights. I not only run races of all lengths—from the 100-yard dash to marathons—but for the past 13 years I have held the World Seniors Boxing Championship and have a standing challenge to climb into the ring with anyone over 65. For the most part, I can't find takers—not in any weight category—so I settle for going three rounds with men in their 40s and 50s.

In addition to these athletic pursuits, my mental processes have never been sharper. I have, in fact, recently obtained patents on three inventions and I am busy planning my next book on how to maintain health.

I also have a very active social life, which often includes ballroom and square dancing with women half my age.

How was I able to start as a physical wreck at 70 and achieve these goals?

A FREAK?

Am I some sort of genetic oddity, the one-in-a-million exception of whom the Philadelphia geriatric specialist spoke?

Is it true, as many segments of the medical profession still maintain, that as we get older it is normal for the body's immune system to become increasingly weak, allowing diseases to take hold and bring us untold suffering and misery?

I don't believe so and there are now respected members of the medical and scientific community who are saying the same thing.

For example, William Adler, M.D., who heads the Gerontology Research Center at the Institute on Aging in Baltimore, Maryland, points to developments in immunology, psychology, exercise, and nutrition. There are now indications, he asserts, that the immune system responds very quickly to adequate nutrition. This is especially true, according to Dr. Adler, when vitamins C and D, as well as iron, are added to the diet.

The April 1985 issue of the *American Journal of Clinical Nutrition* reported on research by two University of Texas nutritionists who found that the dentrils—those thin branching roots that carry electrical impulses from one brain cell to another—can shrivel up and die when there is a lack of B-6 and copper. And the *Journal of the American Medical Association* (June 3, 1983) reported that a husband and wife team of researchers at the University of New Mexico, Jean and John Goodwin, both M.D.s, had discovered that older peoples' capacities decline when they have insufficient amounts of vitamins C, B-12, foliate, and riboflavin.

Dr. Adler also notes that exercise releases a protein that keeps the body's temperature high for several hours after a workout. This is important because body heat fights viruses.

Research at Indiana's Purdue University has shown that when exercise is combined with vitamin supplements, the exertion increases the effects of vitamins C and E. The investigators also found that, whether the person took vitamins or not, the exercise increased the body's production of T (thymus) cells, white blood cells that fight viruses and tumors. The conclusions from this research were that both physical conditioning and greater amounts of vitamins stimulate the immune system.

Chapter One: The Promise

In their 1981 book, *Vitality in Aging,* authors James F. Fries, Ph.D., and Lawrence M. Crapo, Ph.D., both on the faculty of the Stanford University School of Medicine, describe the "rectangular curve," a charting of age versus physical/mental capacity that demonstrates that humans should be able to live a long, vital, and disease-free life. Aging, according to the authors, should not mean the slow, painful downhill slide that I was experiencing until 1970, but a life that can be lived to the fullest.

I agree with these authors, but my contention is more simply stated: Staying healthy and slowing the aging process is achieved by living by the laws of nature.

How do we do this? The following chapters in this book will answer this and other questions.

I also believe that research on improving health and longevity in older people should not focus on trying to prove what makes us sick. Why not, instead, concentrate on finding out how healthy older people are living?

THE AGING TIDE

There is a growing need to take this approach in order to slow down or even reverse the aging process. Every year, greater numbers of Americans reach their 65th birthday. By the year 2000, more than 16 percent of our population—nearly 40 million people—will have passed this milestone. In the next half century, the number will rise to about 55 million. In the past, reaching 65 often signalled a rapid decline into sickly old age. Even if the person managed to "live" another, say, 20 years, few people continued to be productive or creative.

This book is only somewhat of an autobiography. Although it does describe my personal degeneration into a sick old man, why I got that way, and what I did to reverse the damage, it is also a treatise on what *not* to do.

I believe it is time to take a long hard look at the American "good life" that seems to allow this to occur.

In the later chapters I will discuss what I see as the four elements that I believe contain the secret to slowing or even reversing the aging process. These will be the cornerstones of a self-care program. I see such a program as a much-needed step, especially today.

At the beginning of the 20th century, we perhaps had a different form of happiness, knowing each day what our duties would be and working from sunup to sundown. Unfortunately, we also endured many sicknesses, along with calamities such as starvation.

Now, despite all our magnificent technological advances, we still have these unfortunate conditions in many areas of the world. In this respect, we have not made so much progress. But I believe we will come to grips with this situation and begin to make changes.

I am happy to note that more and more people agree that proper diet, moderate intake of food, and lowering stress are among the biggest factors in achieving long life. I also know that the approach described in this book, while quite specific, can produce dramatic changes not only in length but, perhaps more importantly, in quality of life.

As I write this, I am in my 90th year and instead of decreasing my activities, I am increasing them. I know that I have improved much since I was 80, so what I am doing now is enjoying health without a body deficiency.

My hope and prayer is that more people will come to realize that they do not have to be sick, that each individual has within him or her the power to change one's personal future.

May my story be useful to you as a guideline for the young, hope for the middle-aged, and a lifeline for senior citizens. Promise yourself that no matter what your age, you can benefit from adopting this life-style. It is never too late.

Noel at 90!

Chapter Two

THE NOEL JOHNSON OF YESTERDAY

A man is the origin of his action.
—Aristotle, 384–322 B.C.

THE EARLY YEARS

I didn't get to be a dud at 70 overnight. I brought myself to it over many years. In fact, I suspect the roots of my decline reach way back to my childhood.

I was born in the 19th century, July 7, 1899, in the small Minnesota farming community of Heron Lake, population then about 400. My mother, although of sturdy Norwegian stock, was small and frail. Still, she did all the "women's work" on the farm, bore six children, and never complained. My father, also Norwegian but strong and healthy, was both a farmer and a thrasher. That is, he had the equipment to handle not only his own crops but to thrash grain grown by our neighbors.

Our farm at the turn of the century was a wonderful place to grow up. We not only had the clean, fresh country air, but the company of cows, chickens, horses, pigs, sheep, turkeys, ducks, and assorted dogs and cats.

Chapter Two: The Noel Johnson of Yesterday

When I came into this world, life expectancy was about 47 years for a man, slightly longer for a woman. My mother, despite her inborn frailty, lived until 70, my father 10 years more. One of my brothers died in his teens, a second suffered crippling age-related conditions until his death in his 70s. My older brother and two sisters were in poor health for many years.

Farm life was hard, but I believe the continual need for strenuous physical activity was an important factor for those who managed a rather long lifespan.

While we all worked hard, we also ate very well, with plenty of pork roasts, sausages, and bacon as family favorites. Mother set a lavish table and nothing was too good for her growing family. Sugar was considered a good energy food and my parents sure liked sweets. We always had cakes, pies, and cookies for desserts and snacks. White sugar, which we bought in 100-pound sacks, graced the table at every meal. We used it not only on cereals but on other foods as well. My father took a spoonful after each meal, "for energy." We didn't know then about the harmful effects that have been linked to it in recent years.

Fortunately, the long days of hard physical work needed to keep the farm running worked off those excess calories, while the salads, fresh vegetables, fruits, and nuts we consumed helped balance the effects of too much rich meat and my mother's wonderful baking.

Antibiotics were unknown then and the sanitary conditions that commonly prevailed would be unacceptable today. Outhouses were the norm and for hygienic reasons were set at least 50 feet from the house. Mother always seemed to know when one of us had made a trip to that little structure. Invariably, as we clattered back into the house, she had us wash our hands, standing over us to make sure we used the soap.

The old one-speed bicycle often took us to school or town, while providing healthy aerobic exercise along the way. We didn't know then that we were efficiently raising our heart rates and improving our heart and lung capacities, but our bodies benefitted just the same. Nowadays, people are returning to the bicycle as a preferred and beneficial means of transportation and exercise.

In my younger years, my health was generally good and I survived all the usual childhood diseases with reasonable ease. It was not until I was 15 that I faced my first serious illness.

One afternoon, I suddenly felt a terrible pain in my side. My parents called the family doctor, who diagnosed it as indigestion and prescribed medicine for it. I went to bed that evening feeling a little better. Then, about midnight I was awakened with an acute spasm of pain that caused me to cry out in agony.

I was rushed to the hospital, where the doctors found a seriously inflamed appendix that ruptured while I was on the operating table. The doctor told my parents that my chances for survival were not good.

Indeed, the surgical team packed my incision—a hole big enough for a man's fist—with gauze to drain out the pus that was gathering. I lay in that hospital bed for 31 days, as my body slowly conquered the infection and began to heal the wound.

Later, I managed to be "graduated" early from school for fighting with other boys. But then, as we will see, fighting has also played a positive role in my life.

While it is true that I grew up in a relatively healthy environment, I also managed to set the stage for decline into sickly old age by simply doing what everybody else did. My life followed the common pattern. Far from being born a "superman," although a rather healthy and strong teenager, I was nevertheless, and however imperceptibly, on the downward slide.

EARLY ADULTHOOD

By 1919, the United States had entered World War I and my brother Art was an Army motorcycle dispatch driver in France. Patriotism was running high and I wanted to help win the "war to end all wars." But when I tried to enlist, the Army, Navy, and Marines told me that I was too short. Determined and still the fighter, I figured out a way. The Army took me as a volunteer to replace a farm boy who had been exempted from doing work necessary for the war effort.

I went through basic training, but before I could be ordered overseas, Armistice was declared and I was sent home.

I entered a business school in St. Paul and, because I had done a little boxing in the Army, began to hang out at a gym frequented by professional fighters. Soon I was training under a top-notch instructor, who told me I was a natural-born fighter and could make some real money by going on the circuit. I completed my business school classes in 1921 and was offered a job with the Great Northern Railroad. Instead, I took a train home for a wedding date with my love, Zola, a red-headed Scottish lass.

Following our marriage, we both worked for two years on my father's farm before the lure of the West beckoned to us.

We bought a Model-T Ford, outfitted it for sleeping and eating—it just may have been the world's first camper—and started west from Minnesota, intending to settle in the state of Washington.

Five weeks later, we arrived in California's Imperial Valley. The January sun felt so warm and nurturing that we decided Washington could wait. We settled into living in a tent pitched on a vacant lot, and I took a job delivering meat to the nearby towns. A few months later, I found work on a ranch, where I was soon promoted to foreman. With the boost in pay came a two-room house with a large screened porch and, best of all, indoor plumbing.

But lure of the ring was also there. Several of the Mexican laborers who worked for me boxed professionally. My fighting instincts took hold again as I started sparring with them. Eventually, I obtained my own license and would fight once or twice a week, usually in the 126-pound class.

I particularly liked the discipline required for training and keeping in shape. I also liked being a winner.

My daughter, Betty Lou, was born during this time and by 1928, when my parents retired, we had to return home to Minnesota to take over the family farm. Zola and I tried farming for two years, only to decide that we were not meant to till the soil. However, I found that boxing was still in my blood and that even during the Depression years I could make money to help see us through. A six- to ten-round match could bring in $200, although the average fight paid about $50. I fought then in the 135-pound class, ironically the same weight I am today, 60 years later.

Unfortunately, being a boxer in the Midwest meant travel over several states in order to find enough work. Out West, I had plenty of matches only a few miles from home. Also, at this time, Zola's health was declining. And we kept thinking about that warm California sun.

I contacted a friend in El Centro about boxing prospects there. He replied, "You old fool, you're too old to fight," (I was then 33) and promptly offered me a steady job with the Texaco Oil Company. I took it and soon my family was once more settled in the Imperial Valley.

I had been working for Texaco for about a year when I began to have a serious pain in my lower back and a high fever. Again, the doctors initially failed to discover the cause. Finally, they found an abscess on my left kidney that was draining poison into my system. A surgeon had to remove about half the organ to get rid of the abscess. The damage was probably from all those kidney punches I had taken in the ring. Fortunately, such punches are outlawed today.

By 1935, I was promoting midget auto races on the local fairgrounds. I even drove in them, until I had a serious accident and decided I didn't want to go on risking my life that way.

Two years later, the local boxing commissioner and my old fight manager approached me to promote amateur boxing in the local arena. For two years, we held fights every Friday night and drew good crowds. During this time, I trained and managed Manuel Ortiz, who was later to become the World Bantamweight Champion.

I confess I was not exactly a teetotaler in those days and I now shudder to recall that my trademark was an ever-present cigar protruding from my mouth. This was long before the U.S.

Surgeon General's report of the hazards of smoking, but I can testify that at 38 years of age my wind was gone and I could not take part in any roadwork or other physical training for the fighters I managed.

In the late summer of 1939, we moved to San Diego and found a beautiful home only 100 yards from the beach. I applied for a job at the county's largest nonmilitary employer, Convair. I had learned they were not hiring anyone over 40, so I simply rolled back my age a year.

My work was in the jig and fixture department at 55 cents an hour (a weekly paycheck of about $15). It was a good job, but did not allow much physical activity. Soon I was made assistant foreman and found that I had even less chance for exercise. Those were the years of World War II, and we worked seven days a week, 10 hours a day in a poorly ventilated facility, operating in crowded conditions, under stress, and with a noise level that would not be tolerated today. I munched countless doughnuts and other sweets and drank vast quantities of coffee. Breakfast, which I picked up at a coffee shop on the way to work, usually included bacon and eggs and a pastry. Overall, it was certainly not a healthy situation.

And, despite the long work hours, we enjoyed an active social schedule that often included beach parties where food, tobacco, and alcohol were the prime ingredients.

With this life-style, it's no wonder I ended up a roly-poly 170 pounds on my 5 foot 7 inch frame. All that extra weight, coupled with the lack of regular exercise, almost certainly contributed to my uneven heart rhythm in later life.

When I went to work for Convair in 1939, I weighed 130 pounds and was in relatively good health. When I retired from there in 1964, I carried 30 percent more weight. Today, with the advantage of hindsight, I can see that my body probably started to deteriorate about the time I stopped boxing in 1941. During the next 23 years, while I worked hard at my job, there was no longer the urgency to keep in shape and our "average American life-style" included smoking, eating anything and everything I wanted, plus considerable social drinking.

The result was inevitable. There is virtually no way one can ignore the basic laws of nature and not wind up in the condition I found myself at age 65: a complete dud.

Although Zola and I had made many plans for interesting things we wanted to do after I retired, we never got to do them. Neither of us had the energy to leave the house and enjoy the things we wanted to do. Once out of the mainstream of working life, we were retired from everything.

Still, at this time Zola had been asked to help rid the state of pornographic materials and she plunged into an exhausting work schedule that kept her on the go day and night. Her cause was worthy, but worrying over her work took its toll. The series of small strokes that damaged her brain left her in a coma with a diagnosis of senile psychosis.

Zola's illness did not stem from any organic or physical condition. I attribute it to overwork, stress, and worry over the seemingly impossible task of ridding the country of obscene materials for her grandchildren and future generations. She just couldn't accept the daily frustrations she encountered.

Needless to say, this was a very difficult period that took a lot out of me. And I handled it badly. I visited Zola regularly, clinging to the hope that she would one day greet me with that mischievous smile and hold out her arms, but we were denied that miracle. Many times I found it difficult to want to continue with my own life, but the support and encouragement of our children, Betty Lou and Jim, and the delight I found in my great-grandsons held me to life.

Sadly, Zola was mentally lost to us and never recognized or communicated with us again before her passing.

Looking back on that period, I find nothing memorable. I must have spent those 2 1/2 years in a grieving daze, barely managing to function at a minimum level, both mentally and physically. I had no regular activity of any kind and no real reason to leave the house, except for my daily visits to Zola, and she didn't know whether I was there or not. My only consolation was the fact that her condition did not cause her any pain. It helped me greatly to know that at least she wasn't suffering. I watched a lot of television to keep away the despairing thoughts, but I still shuffled aimlessly around the house, eating whatever was at hand and giving no thought to the next day, let alone the next year.

By the time I reached 70, Zola was seriously ill and under a doctor's care, and I was suffering from a half-dozen serious afflictions. I was wallowing in self-pity, telling myself, "Old man, now you're going to be truly alone." I became even more uncaring and apathetic. I realize now that I was simply "waiting" for the next and final stop on my journey of life. I considered I had lived my three score and ten and, in the traditional and conventional sense, my life was over.

I was living alone, eating improperly, and deteriorating daily. One day, my doctor informed me that because my heart would skip a couple of beats every so often I was a high risk for a heart attack. This uneven heart motion may well have been brought on by the extra 35 or so pounds I was lugging around.

Where did that weight come from? A good many of those pounds were certainly the result of decades of what I have been calling my "average American life-style." For me that meant that every day after work I would join my friends at a nearby bar. Our group had a rule: the person who drank the least had to pay.

Well, most of the time I would quit after two beers, so I paid. Those bar bills were probably a very cheap life insurance premium because all the fellows in that drinking group have long since died. As the last of them passed away, I began to think that pretty soon it would be my turn.

You see, even though I stopped at two drinks at the bar, I was not all *that* sensible. I would arrive home, sit down to relax and consume three or four more beers before dinner. On the weekends, it was a six pack a day.

I had begun to drink early in life and during my working years my philosophy was, "Well, what else is there to do? All my friends drink, so I might as well also."

One day, Jim voiced the family's concern and proposed that I go to the hospital for a thorough check-up. It was becoming apparent, he said, that soon I would need someone to look after me, and that would probably mean a nursing home or similar facility. He was right. I certainly wasn't doing a good job of looking after myself.

The following morning, I studied the image that stared at me from the mirror and realized that I not only felt but also looked like an old man. For the first 70 years of my life, I had "followed the pattern" and lived as most people did. Thus, the condition I found myself in at age 70 was probably no different than unnumbered others have faced before me.

After all, it's "normal" to be ill and aging at 70. Isn't this merely the natural progression of events?

Or, is it?

I finally did something I had been carefully avoiding for a long time. I began to think. At first my mind was as rusty and unused as my body, but I persisted and gradually ideas began to form.

I was very clear on what I *didn't* want. I did not want to be bedridden and helpless, a burden to my children. I felt it was still my personal responsibility to take charge of my own life and health, and I wasn't ready to turn that responsibility over to anyone else.

That morning when I stripped down and gazed in the mirror, the image that I saw had all the signs of aging and ill health: a bulging gut, lackluster eyes, unused muscles hanging slack.

I looked defeated.

THE DECISION TO FIGHT BACK

But then I remembered, "Hey, I used to be a fighter." The thought of being "defeated" stirred something in my ego, and here I was about to give up and take the count.

I decided then and there to beat the bell and come out swinging. They can't count you out when you're trying.

The life expectancy figure of 47 years at the turn of the century has been turned around and today is about 74 years. This improvement is due not only to improved antiseptic and sanitary conditions and to the scientific and medical community—which has produced medicines of every sort, plus increasingly complicated diagnostic procedures and equipment—but to great strides made in understanding the workings of the human body and spirit.

However, in many areas and among many age groups, especially the elderly, basic good nutrition is largely ignored, or, where a deficiency is identified, various vitamins are prescribed. People spend many millions of dollars annually on vitamin and mineral supplements, as well as on other so-called "health foods." Still, too many of those who live past retirement age end up in nursing homes or hospitals and are unable to care for themselves.

I choose to be an optimist and believe that at any age we can change our bodies from sickness to health. I did it. And I'm going to lay out the approach you need to take—what to do and what to avoid—to stay physically young while growing chronologically older.

NOELISMS:

The most human instinct is to survive.

If you keep on doing what you have always done, you will keep on being as you have always been.

Noel often enjoys well-known landmarks during his travels. Sydney, Australia.

Chapter Three

HOW I TURNED MY LIFE AROUND

Knowing ignorance is strength; Ignoring knowledge is weakness; If one is sick of sickness, one is not sick.

—Lao Tsu, Sixth Century B.C.

In those early days, when boxing was my avocation, a ring announcer began calling me "Battling Blue Eyes."

The nickname stuck and I remembered it when, at age 71, I began asking myself, "Why do people have to die at 70 years or so?" Finally, I made the decision that I would fight to turn my life around, I would once again be battling, but now I was facing perhaps my toughest opponent ever—myself.

I had viewed that pudgy and haggard figure in the mirror and it seemed to say, "Your first enemy is that extra 35 pounds you are carrying."

I dug out an old pair of tennis shoes, donned a sweat suit, and headed over to the track at the nearby high school. I managed to half walk, half shuffle around the quarter-mile oval, then wearily returned home. I slumped down in a chair. Through the haze of exhaustion, my mind would not let me

Training for Royal Marathon in Bangkok, Thailand.

forget that I had taken a stand that amounted to a monumental shift in my life. I had been letting others do my thinking for me, and look where I was on a steep downhill track toward oblivion. I was just eating, drinking, and existing—and not even doing very well at that.

Now, I concentrated on my thought processes, to get them working for me again. Clearly, while that overweight, flabby body was private enemy number one, my stagnant mind was certainly close behind.

With my muscles crying out in protest from the sudden demand to do some honest exercise, I thought about what it was that goaded me into deciding to make a drastic change in my life-style. I wondered if it was worth it.

At that point, I had strong doubts and it took a lot of "You can do it" affirmations to convince my bewildered mind to keep nagging me not to give up. I would focus on it and think it would be so easy simply to forget the whole plan and just let nature take its course. How strange. Here I was thinking about nature taking its course when, if I had followed natural laws earlier in life, I wouldn't be in this disintegrated condition.

I looked once more in the mirror. Those blue eyes told me, "Giving up is not your style, keep going."

I realized then that the "Don't bother, it's not worth the effort," was my enemy.

To battle this foe, I knew I had to really *want* to make the change. And, the only way I could see doing this was to concentrate on the desired result. I visualized being able to improve my physical condition to the point where I could take care of myself, and perhaps even get into good enough shape that some pretty lass would look at me and think, "There's a man I would like to get to know."

It wouldn't be easy, I reasoned, remembering my aching muscles, but the alternative was grim: to continue to degenerate and become even more disabled than I was. My fighting spirit said, "You're not ready to turn responsibility for your life and well-being over to someone else. And you certainly don't want to be a burden to your family."

The fighter in me triumphed over the "what's the use" part and I decided I was going to be a winner in the ring again—only this ring was inside me and I had both opponents: my aging body and my virtually unused (at least in recent years) mind. I would take control of those brain cells and mobilize them to serve my best interests.

My determination had to be strong enough to direct my mind to discipline my physical activities. And those physical activities were to be done long enough and strong enough to put my body into such a condition that it could perform any action it was asked to do.

I thought about my doctor's fatherly advice, "Take it easy and live longer." Then it occurred to me "Why? So I make more trips to the doctor, and perhaps that final journey to the hospital?" The only benefit I could see was that I would be enriching the doctor's bank account.

So I would exercise. But first, in order to have the strength and stamina to do this, I had to fuel my body properly. Running a mile race while eating "junk food" is like trying to build a brick house on a foundation of soft sand.

I decided that I would begin to eat only natural organic foods, mostly in their raw state. I cut out all meat, white flour, and sugar and munched on pure foods such as dates, raisins, and sesame and sunflower seeds. My rule was simple, if it was green and directly from the earth it became part of my diet: alfalfa, sprouts, lemon leaves, dandelion greens, or whatever.

I stopped having regular meals—those traditional events we call breakfast, lunch, and dinner—and ate only when I was hungry.

I vowed to increase my exercise level steadily. After the first day when I had limped around that high school track, I managed a bit more each day. Within a week, I was able to jog slowly all the way around the oval.

By the end of two years, when I was 72, I had developed a daily run of six to eight miles, which I would normally do on the beach in the early morning. I would follow this with two hours of vigorous calisthenics.

Gradually, my arthritis, bursitis, and gout disappeared. I felt mentally alert and physically refreshed—better, in fact, than I had in many years.

Since I have always been a competitive person, it was only natural that as my running improved I would begin to enter various races.

One of the greatest moments in this part of my return to health came early, when in July 1972, three days before my 73rd birthday, I entered the U.S. Masters Track and Field Championship mile run. It was held in San Diego and, as with all Masters competitions, was open to people over the age of 40.

One of the favorites to win that race was Colonel Dave Fowler. He was about my age and, over the years, had won many Masters gold medals. I did not even consider that I might be able to beat him.

Still, I kept up with him for the first three laps. As we entered the final lap, I was right behind him and only then did I think, "Hey, I just may have the strength to pass him and win." Sure, enough, as we came out of the last turn, I dug into the dirt and managed one last spurt that took me past him. I could hear him behind me panting and blowing out his breath. He was determined to pass me but I just kept running my heart out and crossed the finish line two steps ahead of him.

That win was a tremendous motivator for me. From then on, in each race I would set a goal for myself, either against another runner or against the clock.

It felt wonderful to be a winner again and I was determined not to lose that feeling.

In Chapter One I referred to another "peak" experience—my success in the race up the Colorado mountain named for pioneer explorer Zebulon Pike. This exercise in masochism begins at 6,571 feet and runs up the Barr Trail to the summit at 14,110 feet above sea level. Runners stumble over exposed tree roots, sharp rocks, and baby boulders that test agility and nimbleness. Finally, after fighting a way through the masses of loose stones, runners come to the "golden stairs," 32 switchbacks up the especially steep last thousand feet to the top.

As the oxygen level gets thinner and thinner at higher elevations, the body tries to compensate with rapid and deep breathing, which upsets the balance of oxygen and carbon dioxide in the system and presents the risk of hyperventilation. The result is that after a couple of minutes, runners slow to a staggering walk as their lungs struggle to get enough oxygen.

There is also the danger of what is called mountain sickness, where the symptoms can include headaches, nausea, disorientation, shortness of breath, and—most dangerous of all—edema, with water collecting either in the lungs or brain. Despite these hazards, the first time I ran it I finished second in the Senior (60 and over) Division.

For others who, like myself, are accustomed to the oxygen-rich air at sea level, I suggest coming to the mountain a week or two ahead of time to train at a camp at the 8,500 foot level staffed with instructors who specialize in high altitude athletics. I intend to run the Pike's Peak Marathon again next year—at age 90.

I must admit that another thrill was to be picked, at age 75, to appear on five million *Wheaties* cereal boxes in their "Breakfast of Champions" series.

I also had fun the following year stumping the panel on the television show *To Tell the Truth*. Master of Ceremonies Joe Garagiola asked the panel to identify the "superman" among the three people seated before them. I got only one vote—from a New York sports writer who thought he detected a cauliflower ear on my head. He was right.

Then in 1981, I was thrilled to be on the *CBS Evening News* with Dan Rather, who had learned I was entered in my second New York Marathon. Competing in those races has brought out a "running" banter between New York Mayor Ed Koch and myself. A few years ago, His Honor greeted me with, "Johnson, I'm going to get you for fraud. You're not 85 or you wouldn't be running these races. I'm 58 and I can't do it."

The following year, I was interviewed by Richard Simmons for his national television health and fitness show. This intelligent young man is an incredible dynamo of energy, and it is exciting just to be around him.

THE TRAINING TABLE

I ran that New York Marathon in 1981 without much training. Since then, I have learned a lot about racing and I have refined my training technique. One area that I am especially careful about is eating properly before a race. Before most marathons, the runners are served a dinner rich in carbohydrates, normally spaghetti. It is expected that all serious runners will have this meal. I don't. I think the benefits of spaghetti are overrated.

I do not believe you can condition your body in the few hours before a major race. In fact, I worked hard for two solid years before I felt ready to enter a race.

There is another myth concerning food that I want to discuss: the belief that downing a sugary drink, or taking sugar, while exercising will boost your stamina and ward off fatigue. True, your blood sugar levels may fall during strenuous exercise but simply dumping sugar into the system will not provide the extra energy to run, say, another few miles in a marathon. What in fact happens is your insulin level rises and you feel more hungry. Also, the sugar is burned up rapidly, so any energy you receive is short lived.

A study in the *New England Journal of Medicine* reported on research conducted in England on 19 men who worked out on stationary bicycles until they were physically exhausted. They were then given sugar water to drink. Their blood was tested and while the blood-sugar levels remained high, the sugar they had consumed did not improve the length of time they could exercise. The study did determine that although low blood sugar was common during the later stages of the exercise, the participants were still able to continue the exercise for between 15 to 70 minutes more.

For me, running is a large part of my self-care program. I run for my health. I run in races because I thrive on the competition. I truly believe that running not only prolongs life, but it improves the quality of it by conditioning the body for every sort of physical activity.

IMPROVING MY STATE OF AFFAIRS

During the first couple of years of my rejuvenation program I was totally wrapped up in getting my body and mind into fine condition. As this took place, I gradually began to sense that something was missing. I was feeling restless and a bit uneasy—but did not know why. Then it struck me. I had been living alone for several years but at heart I had always been a sociable person. Before my wife suffered her strokes, we had enjoyed an active social life with my family and friends and I especially liked talking with women acquaintances.

Now, here I was, a widower and alone. Then I thought, "But who would be interested in a 73-year-old man?"

One day, after a run, I was feeling tired and on my way home passed a massage studio. This particular establishment did not have the unsavory reputation that many do. I sought and received a legitimate muscle massage.

I might add that I normally run without a shirt, so my skin is usually well tanned from the California sun. At the same time, it can be somewhat dry.

As I passed the massage establishment, I thought, "How relaxing it would be just to lie down and have warm oil rubbed into my skin."

When I arrived home, I called for an appointment, showered and changed, then went to have my massage.

The masseuse, an attractive woman in her early 30s named Linda, showed me to a room and asked what type of massage I wanted. I explained that warm oil would feel really good. She had me remove my clothes and lie on my stomach. She then proceeded to massage me from head to toe. I could feel my dry skin literally drinking in the oil.

She asked me how I managed to have such a good tan. I told her about my running and she commented that I had a much better physique than most men who came in.

We talked and she told me that her husband had left her a few years earlier, that she was now divorced and was raising a seven-year-old daughter.

I really enjoyed not only the massage but also the conversation with Linda. I made a second appointment the following week. I found that I was really looking forward to that massage. And when I arrived, Linda appeared really glad to see me again. Although she was quite proper and formal in her work, I couldn't help but think how nice it would be if I could hold her in my arms. But she would never allow that, I told myself.

Thoughts of Linda kept coming to mind in the following days and finally I got up enough nerve to ask her if she would have dinner with me some evening. To my surprise and delight she accepted. She said she had not had a dinner date in several years. We arranged to go out on her day off.

When I arrived at her home that night, I was happy to see how pretty she looked. I was proud to be with her.

We talked a great deal during dinner and afterward we drove back to her apartment, where I met her daughter and an older woman with whom she shared the dwelling.

I asked her for another date, to dinner and the theater. During the evening, I asked her if she would come to my home on her day off and give me a massage. She said she would be happy to do so, but refused to take any payment for the service.

When we were alone in my room, it seemed I was massaging her as much as she was me. And, it had to happen: the next step was to make love.

She was willing, but I found I was unable to carry out my part of the proceedings. Until then, I had thought I could make love any time I wanted to, although it had been several years since I had been with a woman.

So, here I was with a beautiful young lady wanting me to make love to her—and I was a dud.

While I was apologetic and embarrassed, Linda remained patient and understanding. "Next time it would be all right," she said, adding that I must be "out of practice."

Out of practice!

The comment stuck in my mind. I thought of the phrase popular with people who are strong on exercise and even among some doctors: "Use it or lose it."

That was it; if I did not practice running, I would grow rusty and unable to perform in a race or on the track.

Was it the same with sex?

It seemed logical that here, too, a person must stay in condition. One must be in good physical condition to run long distances and this includes the proper nutrition. I started reading whatever I could find—and there is not too much—on the subject of foods needed for sexual potency. Throughout history, various types of edibles have been touted as being "the one" for this purpose. Aphrodisiacs are reputed to include such things as oysters, red peppers, and soft- and hard-boiled eggs, among others. It seemed to me that the best food would be one that has the most sex hormones, and I found that honeybee pollen fits this bill.

While "next time" proved to be a bit longer than Linda and I had thought, there was steady improvement and finally complete success. Linda and I shared an intimate companionship for many years.

Actress Mae West once said, "It's not the men in my life that counts, it's the life in my men."

I have proven that I have a lot of life in me and I intend to continue this happy "state of affairs."

I have enjoyed warm and sexually satisfying relationships with other women, but a gentleman—even a stud in his late 80s—does not provide chapter and verse details.

Now just months away from my 90th birthday, I do not spend a nickel on medication. I am able to participate in long-distance running, championship boxing, ballroom dancing, and whatever else catches my fancy.

I have proven that whatever a person wants to do can be accomplished if the body and mind are in accord. Moreover, I also know that being in physical condition by itself does not guarantee success at making love. However, the overall answer is total conditioning of mind and body. I believe that the soul knows no age. It is in our minds that we decide we are too old to do this or that activity. The mind, faced with a life filled with monotony, tells the body, "Don't bother." The result is laziness and apathy. There is a simple sequence that lets you escape from this prison of ennui. Fantasize what you want, then put your mind to work to create what you have dreamed.

NOELISM:

Lord, I confess I am not what I ought to be, but thank you Lord that I am not what I used to be.

Back in the Race Again

The horizons of my life have expanded immeasurably in the past two decades, not only in physical activity and personal relationships but in my daily life. I have traveled the world talking to people about my life and how I live it. Health and longevity are of great interest to me and this seems to be a subject of interest to a lot of other people.

For this reason, just let me list some of the things I did in 1987. In April I went to Iceland to lecture on my philosophy. I made personal appearances at an 11-day world exposition and competed in a 7K run. By summer things really got busy. In late August I went back to Iceland for more appearances, then on to Norway. In Sweden, together with 35,000 other runners, I ran a half marathon. I did the same thing in Denmark, and in Finland ran a one-hour race that started at 11 p.m., while it was still daylight in the artic summer.

While in Finland, I visited a sanitarium—a health center—for three days of tests. They pronounced me in excellent health. I returned to the United States and prepared for further trips abroad later in the year.

On November 1, I ran my sixth New York Marathon. (As readers will recall, I had run my first one eight years earlier, at the age of 80.) It was exciting to find that now, nearing 90, I could still finish the 26.2 mile course. I returned from New York to pack for a trip to Singapore. The 12,000-mile, 21-hour flight was tiring, and when I arrived my hosts had arranged for me to fly to a half dozen other Asian countries to talk about my program of rejuvenation and my views on health and nutrition.

Then, on November 22, just three weeks after completing the grueling New York Marathon, I completed the Royal Marathon in Bangkok, Thailand, running in 90-degree temperatures with high humidity.

I was treated royally all along the way, attending parties for the daughter of the king, the prime minister, and other high officials of the Thai government.

My visit in Thailand stirred articles in all of Bangkok's daily newspapers, plus radio and television coverage.

Then, in early December, I flew to Australia, where I was busy from morning to night, accepting interviews, disco dancing, as well as entering a two-round exhibition boxing match with that country's featherweight and bantamweight champion, Jeff Fennech.

In mid-December, I took the long flight home to San Diego, via Tahiti, and later that month went to Minneapolis to get ready for a family get-together with my nine great-grandchildren, including the first girl of that generation, Lily Noelle.

Chapter Four

HOW TO CURE IMPOTENCE

What pipes and timbrels? What wild ecstacy?
—John Keats, 1795–1821

Let's start by dispelling a myth.

We are led to believe that sex is not good unless it involves extended foreplay, long-and-drawn-out intercourse, followed by a simultaneous, volcanic, fireworks-generating orgasm—Hemingway's "the earth moved" sort of thing—followed by a period of complete exhaustion by both partners.

Books, magazines, movies, and folklore promote this scenario—which is not to say it does not happen—but realize also that the level of sensations and feelings can vary from Keats' "wild ecstacy" to lesser, but still very satisfying, warmth and pleasure.

The point is that so many men and women are still locked into the myths of performance and level of experience.

When one partner does not reach these levels, or feels he or she has not perfomed up to expectations, there are often feelings of frustration, guilt, inadequacy, and, perhaps worst of all, anxiety. Or, maybe one partner isn't in the mood at a given time. Again, there is the potential for anger, resentment, blaming, and more. Such feelings can be a major cause of temporary impotence in men or of a woman's inability to achieve an orgasm.

What is needed is a loving understanding that we are all human and at times temporarily subject to less-than-optimum physical or mental conditions. Couple this with the belief that "the next time will be better." But what about when that time, and the next, and the next are not better?

Conservative estimates indicate that at least 10 million American men (about one in every nine) experience one of the following embarrassing dilemmas: failure to achieve an erection, early fading of one just before or just after penetration, or premature ejaculation. It is also true that about 25 percent of all American men over age 65 suffer from impotence, and that by the time a man reaches his 70s and 80s the percentage rises sharply.

Impotence in men and the inability to achieve orgasm in women can be the result of physical or psychological causes, or a combination of the two.

PHYSICAL PROBLEMS

Among the physical causes of impotence are disease, anatomical changes, and hormonal shifts, while psychological triggers can range from guilt or shame to anger or simple strained relations with one's partner.

Diseases that can cause impotence include diabetes, where the odds of becoming impotent are as much as five times that of the non-diabetic; high blood pressure; bladder, kidney or liver failure; prostate and bowel surgeries; testicular problems; back and spinal cord injuries; hardening of the arteries; and poor circulation and nervous system disorders such as Parkinson's disease and multiple sclerosis.

At times, even medicine prescribed for an altogether different physical or mental ailment is to blame. Medications that alleviate high blood pressure, depression, and ulcers can produce side effects that include a lower libido. However, even with such more-or-less drastic physical conditions, impotence is not a given. In many cases, sexual potency continues.

IT'S NOT HOW OLD YOU ARE

One very important point: Age does not cause impotence. If a man, for instance, maintains good physical and mental health, he most likely can enjoy sex through his entire life.

As the years move on, however, certain gradual changes do take place. A full erection may not be quite as firm as when the man was 20, and the volume and force of the ejaculation may be somewhat less. Also, the period of recovery—the moment of time it takes for him to become erect again—may be longer.

You may be thinking, "But the quantity of sex has decreased." This may be true, but in many cases the quality has increased. In fact, older people, who no longer have the pressures of career, raising children, and other family-life demands may find that they can now make love more often and in a more relaxed fashion that actually allows a greater degree of closeness. The experiences, while not the same as in the twenties, can still be rich and satisfying.

HOW OFTEN?

People wonder what the normal frequency is for making love. Anywhere from twice a day to once a month—or even more or less frequently—is not abnormal. It depends on the individuals involved and to a great degree on keeping one's body healthy.

Furthermore, adequate nutrition, which includes vitamins, minerals, enzymes, coenzymes, and hormones, is vital to the healthy functioning of all the body's parts, including the reproductive system. I believe that those plant foods in nature that are created to fertilize and reproduce—such as bee pollen (see Chapter Eight) and live seeds that are prepared to germinate—are what the human body needs to continue the regeneration and, in this case, the reproductive process.

PSYCHOLOGICAL PROBLEMS

"It's all in your mind" is a convenient way to dismiss and even try to explain away a man's inability to get an erection. However, as science has learned, these problems are *not* all in the mind. Indeed, they are actually a psychological and chemical double whammy.

It all goes back to very ancient times and involves the autonomic (automatic) nervous system, which we will discuss in more detail in Chapter Ten. For now, the important thing to remember is that frequently the cause of impotence is anxiety, stress, or fear—fear of failure or fear of poor performance.

Fear of poor performance, for the man, can involve his wondering, "Am I going to get it up?" or "Will my technique be as good as that of her previous partner?" or "Can I bring her to orgasm?"

The man then becomes frustrated, upset, and perhaps angry with himself. The result is that emotions simply compound the reaction in the body and *nothing* happens.

Soon, he may begin to think, "Hey, there must be something physically wrong with my apparatus." Thus, at the moment of every failure, he becomes more and more convinced that "It isn't in my mind, no sir." He's right, because by then the chemical process of the adrenalin reflex has taken place.

Respected, nationally known sex therapist Dr. Theresa Crenshaw, M.D., in her book *Bedside Manners—Your Guide to Better Sex*, explains what happens during the adrenalin reflex.

THE ADRENALIN REFLEX

Recent research has shown that a chemical triggered by fear causes loss of erection. The process is related to the body's "fight-or-flight" response (see Chapter Ten), where glands generate the "survival" chemical adrenalin and pump it into the bloodstream to prepare the person for combat or escape. To gear the body up for these alternatives, the body's release of adrenalin brings about a number of physiological changes. Included among them is restriction of the blood vessels in all the periphery areas, including the penis, in order to concentrate the vital substance deep in the body's core. This way blood can be instantly available in the event of injury or to carry energy to muscles for rapid flight.

The important point is that this reaction is a virtually instantaneous response when fear or stress is felt. The body doesn't wait to figure out whether the fear or stress is physical or psychological, real or imagined. It simply goes immediately into action to be ready for the worst.

So, how can fear intervene just at the critical juncture when intercourse is about to begin? Dr. Crenshaw likens the reaction to the one felt by the matador at the "moment of truth."

He is facing the bull at close range preparing to reach over the animal's horns to plunge the blade of his sword into the precise spot required for a clean kill. If he misses the mark, or if the bull moves suddenly, he could be seriously injured. Here comes the adrenalin.

The man who has trouble drawing his wife to orgasm worries each time that he will fail. Or, for whatever reason, he does fail once. From then on, he worries, "Will it happen again?" The more he worries, the more stressful sex becomes and the more likelihood there is that he will trigger the release of adrenalin.

The adrenalin reflex also can trigger premature ejaculation, which in certain situations may have nothing to do with erotic thoughts but with fear. (Men about to be executed have suddenly ejaculated.)

WHAT WON'T HELP?

Dr. Crenshaw points out that one route people take, downing a few drinks beforehand to stiffen the resolve by relaxing anxiety, may be counterproductive. Perhaps a drink or two by the light drinker may "short-circuit" the adrenalin reflex, but it is not a good idea to become dependent on alcohol because it is a chemical depressant which will, in the long run, decrease the ability to become erect.

Shakespeare is reputed to have advised that alcohol provokes desire but takes away performance. Another way to put it plays upon a popular concept: "A loaf of bread, a jug of wine, and forget about the thou."

Negative feelings about yourself can also do you in, says Crenshaw, who cites as an example the student facing an exam who says, "I'm going to fail anyway, so what's the use?" As a result, he or she procrastinates before starting to study and, once finally settled down to try to review notes or the textbook, can't concentrate. A self-fulfilling prophesy is about to happen.

If, on the other hand, the student—or, in our case, the lover—says to himself, "I'm not going to think about the past, but I'll concentrate instead on the present and give it my best shot," that "shot" may be fine.

By all means, avoid saying to yourself, "Don't think about it." Consider what happens if someone tells you, "Don't think about crocodiles." The first image that comes to mind is, of course, one of large reptiles.

Wouldn't it be far better to tell yourself some fascinating sexual story? Then see how fast those crocodiles are forgotten.

Then there is the "negative spectator." This, explains Crenshaw, is when a part of the man (or woman) is looking in from a point outside the experience and judging performance.

Man: I don't seem to be getting very erect.

Woman: I'm not getting very aroused, this isn't going to work."

This, too, becomes a self-fulfilling prophecy.

WHAT MAY HINDER THAT RESPONSE?

Believe it or not, one's notion of what love is can be a defeating factor in lovemaking. For the man, there can be the so-called "madonna-whore syndrome."

By its nature and its name, sex must be sexual. That is, it must be erotic to cause arousal. Thus, if a person's idea of what constitutes love is defined only in terms of, say, purity and light—with no room for the erotic—then when the loved person is present those feelings block out any erotic images and prevent any erotic acts. Without the erotic element, there is no arousal and the sexual performance can't commence.

Dr. Crenshaw adds a small but important bit of wisdom for women who wonder about their man's feelings during sex: Recognize that some men are able to function precisely because their emotions are *not* involved at that time. They are simply enjoying themselves.

WIDOWER'S SYNDROME

As I described in the previous chapter, my beloved Zola's health failed over a period of years. Of course I did not approach her sexually during that time. After she was gone, and I had suffered through my period of grieving, I began to make the first tentative steps toward establishing a loving relationship with another woman. But, when the moment of intimate contact arrived, I found—as I have described—that the period of disuse had taken its toll and I could not automatically begin sexual activities. Fortunately, with time and an understanding partner, I was able to overcome this problem.

But suppose when this first happened I had said to myself, "Well, that's it, I'm over the hill. Forget about sex."

As an analogy, suppose I had broken my arm and had to have it in a cast for six weeks. When that cast was removed, I would find that I did not have the full range of motion I had before. But, with exercise, my arm would gradually regain its ability to function completely.

It seems that we tend to put the sex act in a separate category from other bodily actions and functions. If we accept the fact that sexual performance is one of the body's natural functions, we can do away with much of the belief that different rules somehow apply with lovemaking.

WHAT CAN HELP

Clearly, positive feelings can be crucial to getting back on the sexual track. The same approach of positive reinforcement applies to spectatoring. Instead of chastising yourself by cataloging the things you may be doing wrong, why not look instead at your partner and see that person enjoying sex with you.

SET THE MOOD

Make use of the power of suggestion to put you and your partner in the right frame of mind. Just as shedding a little light on the subject or using mirrors can add to the erotic effect, there are other mood-setting tactics that also can help. Use soft lights or a few small candles, romantic music, incense, a comfortable setting, a fire in the fireplace—anything that will appeal to the five senses. Be aware of the songs or instrumental music that arouses you—even chamber music or symphonies might transport you to the heights. If you enjoy the sounds of the sea, perhaps a tape of ocean waves will carry you into the mood. Many people enjoy the sounds of a rainy night, whether live or taped.

And don't forget the sense of smell. If you're not into incense, perhaps perfume and after-shave lotion will stimulate arousal. The guidelines to setting the mood are based on what pleases *you*.

VISUALIZE SUCCESS

Whatever the sport or activity in which you wish to succeed, you must concentrate on what you want to accomplish. Our minds must be attuned to what we want to achieve. The same is true for sexual intercourse. If you have experienced any sexual problems, perhaps visualizing success and satisfaction will help. Devote half an hour each day to thinking about sex—what arouses you most and what pleases you most. Use whatever thoughts you must to stimulate your sexual appetite. Successful athletes use visualization techniques during their conditioning and before their races. Consider yourself as an athlete in a different sport. You may even find that by setting the mood and by using the power of suggestion, the senario described at the beginning of this chapter might well come true.

Finally, keep in mind that throughout life, people can respond to and enjoy sexual intimacy, with its closeness, touching, and other pleasures.

So go ahead and light those candles.

Chapter Five

GET ON THE PATH

> *Better to hunt in fields for health unbought,*
> *than fee the doctor for a nauseous draught.*
> *The wise for cure on exercise depend;*
> *God never made his work for man to mend.*
>
> —John Dryden, 1631–1700

So many middle-aged people say to me, "Why shouldn't I keep on with my present life style? I feel fine."

My answer to them is, "I'm glad you're feeling fine today, but what will you be like in 10 years? To get an idea, look back 10 years and see what you could do then that you no longer can do now."

I had not thought too much about my own downhill slide until, at age 71, I suddenly became painfully aware of what had happened to me. I realized then that aging effects are cumulative. Fortunately, I also found out that the human body can take a lot of punishment and still bounce back—if one starts giving it consistently good care. And such care is not something you do now and then in your spare time. It requires a commitment that you follow on a regular and ongoing basis.

That is why I say, no matter what your age, unless you adopt a self-care program and make the commitment to yourself to carry it out, the next 10 years will take as much, and maybe more, out of you as the last 10 did. I call adopting such a program "getting on the path" to a better life.

We know from scientific studies that the body can restore itself. Think of the way we heal wounds and recover from illness. This happens because our immune system is working hard to help the healing process by directing monocytes (large white blood cells) to fight infection and by making platelets in the blood to clump together to stop bleeding so the cells can begin the rebuilding process.

The immune system also communicates with the disease-fighting B Cells (white blood cells that multiply rapidly to fight invaders called antigens) and T cells (cells programmed by the thymus gland to fight bacteria and tumors).

This restoration process takes place throughout the body—including the brain.

However, we also know that as people get older their immune systems become weaker. That's because the major control device for the system, the thymus gland, ages faster than other organs.

A great deal of current research is concerned with developing ways to strengthen the immune responses of those with lung cancer or chronic hepatitis. Only in recent years have molecular biologists been able to duplicate minute protein substances to boost the strength of the immune system. The investigators hope that soon these approaches can be applied to cancer, AIDS, infectious diseases, and even autoimmune diseases, where the body's defenders mistake a part of the body for an invading enemy and attack it, such as with rheumatoid arthritis.

While our immune system is getting valuable help from medical science, it is up to us to provide the final line of defense by doing all we can individually to keep this system strong.

PEOPLE HAVE EXCUSES

There are always people who will tell you they are unable to take on a self-care program that involves making life-style changes. They think they have good reasons, such as, "It's too late," "I could never do all those things," "You can't teach an old dog new tricks," and so on. Being a doubter may seem to be the easy answer, but such an attitude prevents progress. We've all seen instances of pessimists putting down an idea that later turned out to be correct.

This classic example illustrates my point well. In the early days of this century, when the first cars began appearing on our roads, some people were saying, "It's no use trying to develop this machine because man cannot be moved faster than 15 miles per hour. If he travels at a greater speed, he won't be able to breathe." Today, of course, we go faster than that on a bicycle.

I happen to believe the adage that, "The optimist may be wrong but he has a lot more fun than the pessimist."

THE SELF-CARE APPROACH

I am convinced that we were created to live a life of health, and so we were given our immune defense system to help keep us that way. But we can't rely on the immune system to do it all because, as we have seen, without help it gets progressively weaker. And, while relatives and other loved ones may sincerely want to provide for us, in the long run only we are really responsible for the quality of the life we lead.

On the other hand, just as we are ultimately responsible for our condition, so we can, by our life-style, prevent our defense system from doing its job effectively.

In this chapter, I introduce the basic elements of my self-care program: **Nutrition, Exercise, Breathing**, and **Mind Control,** which not only constitute a quartet of ways to aid the immune system, but allow you to have more fun and live a longer, happier life. Each will be covered individually and in detail in succeeding chapters. Let's consider why these areas are so important.

Exercise

Dr. George Sheehan, author of the best-selling books, *Running and Being* and *Dr. Sheehan on Fitness*, talks about the benefits of exercise and how fitness raises the quality of life, not the quantity. "We acquire zest and energy and vitality to face the day with confidence and enthusiasm. We produce creative energy to let us be free and spontaneous in problem solving."

Those who say, "I simply don't have the time to become fit" should realize, says Sheehan, that a fitness program, by increasing your energy level, actually produces *more* productive time. He points out that being fit allows one to accept the Olympic idea: FARTHER, FASTER, HIGHER.

In my own case, the exercise that has been my route to rejuvenation is running. The opportunity to develop as a runner came thanks to the U.S. Masters Track and Field Championships. The Masters have helped countless "has beens" get up off our posteriors and live a healthful, vigorous life again. People from 40 to 80 and above have been inspired to get in shape through these events. I am greatly indebted to Masters founder Dave Payne and the others who put on these meets, because without them I probably would not have taken the time and put the energy into training to compete against others in many interesting places, and I would not have met so many wonderful people.

There is as yet no evidence to show that exercise itself will prevent or cure any disease, even heart problems. What exercise does do, however, is add life and happiness and build up one's self-image.

Being fit, in short, allows one to function at a higher level of development, to shove back the barriers of fatigue, exhaustion, shortness of breath, and pain which limit our lives. We will examine the topic of exercise in the following chapter.

Nutrition

Like many people in this country, I believe that for many of us eating is not only a habit, but an addiction we must control in order to keep our bodies in good health.

The recent U.S. Surgeon General's report on nutrition, disease, and mortality in America bears this out. It noted that 34 million adult Americans are overweight, and that 71 percent of the two million people who died in 1987 succumbed to diseases associated with diet. The report pointed out that coronary heart disease, stroke, atherosclerosis, diabetes, and some cancers are influenced by what we eat.

Not the least of the matter is that 10 percent of us (about 24 million people) have high blood pressure—usually referred to as hypertension—with its risk of prolonged illness and early death.

All this is frightening but it is also profoundly sad. The fact is, life does not have to end prematurely. We have the natural apparatus to live a long, healthy, and productive existence.

As William A. McGarey, M.D., Founder and Director of the A.R.E. Medical Clinic in Phoenix, Arizona, has observed, "Pathologists tell us that the only way to die is by accident or illness. If one stays healthy, one hardly has time to develop any illness. We are really more in control of what happens to our bodies than we suspect or act out."

Research has shown that what we eat can influence the functioning of the immune system. Those nutrients that specifically influence our level of disease fighters include:

fatty acids—found in polyunsaturated fats, where an excess inhibits T cell response (a teaspoon of vegetable oil a day gives us enough)

vitamin A—one carrot every 3-4 days provides a sufficient supply

vitamin E—a deficiency or a surplus can reduce the effectiveness of the immune response

vitamin B-6

pantothenic acid

folic acid

vitamin C

minerals, especially iron, where again a deficiency is bad while too much helps bacteria and parasites to multiply

zinc

copper

selenium

and **iodine.**

Breathing

One of the paths that leads us to lower stress levels involves developing our power of positive concentration. Phil Nuernberger, Ph.D., writing in the October 1985 issue of *Elle Magazine,* noted that concentration comes in two forms—negative and positive. The first is brought into focus by outside stimulation—fear and stress are examples. This type of concentration produces "tunnel vision."

Positive concentration results from calm and release from those outside disturbances. Nuernberger advocates practicing a simple process of *breath awareness* to build our ability for voluntary concentration. This process, he contends, allows us to have a clearer mind, one that lets us get in touch with our inherent creativity and intuition. We will discuss this breathing technique in Chapter Nine.

Indeed, breathing only from the lungs is a short and shallow effort. Deep breathing—all the way from the diaphragm—not only reduces tension and increases our concentration but provides added oxygen the body needs. Try inhaling for a full seven seconds; you should feel the air filling the space from the abdomen to your upper chest. Then exhale slowly and evenly for eight seconds.

Mind Power

Finally, there is that powerful player in your contest for health—the mind. It plays a major role in how we perform, but many people underestimate what it can do for them. If we convince ourselves by thinking negatively that we will fail at a task, we are defeated at the outset. On the other hand, if we start to reach out to improve our physical health, our determination—bolstered by the mind's saying "Go for it, you can do it"—is a positive force toward success. We will explore the power of the mind in Chapter Ten.

STICK WITH IT

Unfortunately, it seems that most people who start a self-improvement program quit after only a few weeks. That seems short-sighted. After all, when you are dealing with your quality of life, shouldn't it be a life-long commitment?

A *U.S. News and World Report* fitness guide cited American Sports Data, Inc., research indicating that most people who begin a fitness program do not keep at it at least two days a week. In 1987, researchers asked a sampling of people who started an exercise program if, 100 days later, they were still exercising. The results indicated that, of the 23 million people who began walking for fitness, 10 million did not stick with it for at least the prescribed time. Similarly, of the 28.7 million who climbed on a bicycle, only 2.6 million were still on a regular peddling program at the end of 100 days. Among the 22.9 million who chose swimming, only 2.6 million continued going to the pool regularly. And, less than a quarter of the 32.9 million who took up running or jogging kept it up for more than the three and one-third months.

We don't know why these people did not keep up their exercise. Some probably had unrealistic expectations for how fast they could get in shape. Maybe no one told them that with physical conditioning, as with so many of life's endeavors, there are no "instant success" methods. It takes time and a fair amount of hard work.

I can guess, too, that perhaps they are not using their minds to motivate themselves to keep going. The process can be as simple as allotting a specific part of one's day several times a week for exercise and, when that time arrives, telling yourself, "Well, let's go, it's time to work on my well-being." And, when you are out there sweating through your exercise routine and wondering why on earth you continue to put up with this "torture," remind yourself to "Keep at it—my life is worth the effort."

On the other hand, even for the dedicated exerciser, following the "no pain, no gain" philosophy is usually not a good idea. That's because going until you hurt can result in overuse injuries that may sideline you for a month or more. A better motto to follow is, "No effort, no gain."

That effort should be based on realistic expectations. San Diego sports therapist Ozzie Gontang, who conducts a clinic to teach people how to run marathons, cautions,

> Too many people focus on excellence to the point where they feel they have to be "the best," as opposed to being "the best me," which may mean never running an Olympic marathon. A great many people who talk about getting fit never ask, "Fit for what?" What they really are saying is "Fit for life."

Your success in a particular sport could rest to some extent on whether you are a man or woman. Men, on the average, tend to have larger hearts—weighing about 10 ounces compared to the womens' which average around 8 ounces—so they can pump more blood and utilize more oxygen. Thus, a man may be able to run distances more easily than a woman. On the other hand, women, because they have a higher percentage of body fat—averaging 28 percent to 18 percent for men—have greater buoyancy in water, so generally it is easier for them to become better swimmers.

Those who are interested in muscle strengthening may hear about a device said to aid muscle movement by providing a mild electric jolt (between 20 and 50 volts of current). Such electrical stimulation training (the effect is said to be like a vigorous massage) is now being evaluated by doctors who see a possible benefit with patients who must remain immobile following surgery.

At least one doctor has commented that while applying such current may provide a moderate amount of muscle strengthening in people who can't otherwise move their muscles, so far there appears to be little or no evidence of strengthening among those whose muscles operate in normal day-to-day activities.

THE FOUNTAIN OF YOUTH?

Doctors Fries and Crapo, in their *Vitality in Aging,* note that the myth of the "fountain of youth" has recurred through history. The myth probably first appeared about 5000 years ago with the epic story told by the Babylonians of their King Gilgamesh and his search for eternal life and youth with a rose-like plant said to grow at the bottom of earth's deepest sea. It appeared again about 700 B.C. in the fable of the Hindu priest Cyavana. The ancient Hebrews, Greeks, and Romans had similar stories and the legend surfaced again in 1513, when Ponce de León accidentally found Florida. The researchers emphasize that there is no solid evidence to date of any human being living more than about 120 years. They also observe that in the 1930s, data began to accumulate indicating that perhaps by lowering the caloric level in our diets, we might prolong life. The experiments subjected laboratory rats to a diet containing few calories but ample protein, vitamins, and minerals.

Results showed that the life span of these animals was not only prolonged but that they continued to appear young and did not become afflicted with chronic diseases until late in their lives.

Today, UCLA researcher Dr. Roy Walford (age 63) is working along the same lines and is using himself as a human subject. Walford is studying the effects of restricting calories (1,500 a day--half the national average) and of eating higher levels of carbohydrates and proteins. His objective is not merely to live longer but to maintain vitality in old age.

What all this indicates is that while perhaps our maximum life span cannot be prolonged, maybe the period of an active and rewarding life can.

Through the years, a number of well-known people have proven to themselves that an individually tailored self-care program--even when started late in life--can bring back or prolong the healthy years.

One who established such a program is the glamorous television and supper club entertainer with only one name,

Hildegarde. In her 1962 book *Over 50--So What?*, this delightfully frank individual describes her secrets of staying youthful, vital, and useful. Her approach, while perhaps somewhat less scientific than Walford's, produced insights worth considering today.

On the subject of diet, Hildegarde declared,

> We eat, it seems to me, those foods upon which our imagination is most likely to dwell. Which is a roundabout way of saying that our eating habits start in our mind. If, therefore, we can train ourselves to associate fattening food with the heavy feeling and the bulges it produces, it will come to be less tempting. Contrarily, if we can train ourselves to associate nourishing and nonfattening food with a feeling of well-being, an attractive slimness, smooth skin, clear eyes and healthy hair, it will come to be more tempting.

Hildegarde had a great many other habits which today we know are vital for good health, including such things as cutting down on sodium (and instead using celery, ocean, or Vege-salt), drinking a glass of carrot juice to quell hunger pangs between meals, and cutting out over-refined products in favor of natural ones.

Elsewhere in her book, she offers this cogent comment: "Normally our bodies serve us well even when we abuse them. We are strong mechanisms, designed for survival. But when we break nature's laws, almost always, sooner or later, we pay a penalty."

She cites a quotation attributed to scientist-philosopher (and 1912 Nobel Laureate) Dr. Alexis Carrel which is especially worth repeating in these times: "If the doctor of today does not become the dietician of tomorrow, the dietician of today will become the doctor of tomorrow."

Then there are the words attributed to the "father of western medicine," Hippocrates in 400 B.C.:

"Leave thy drugs in the chemist's pot
if thou canst heal the patient with food."

My four-part self-care program is designed to work within nature's laws. For I believe, like Hildegarde, that if we don't upset mother nature, she won't upset us.

To continue on the path, read on. There's more to be learned about Exercise, Nutrition, Breathing, and Mind Power.

And, may the force (of nature) be with you.

Known as "Batlin Blue Eyes" in boxing circles, Noel still boxes and holds world titles in his age category.

Chapter Six

EXERCISE—GET YOUR BODY MOVING

Keep the Faculty of Effort Alive in You by a Little Gratuitous Exercise Every Day.

—William James, 1842–1910

The World Health Organization (WHO) defines health as not just the absence of disease but as a state of complete physical, mental, and social well-being. Exercise, along with nutrition and other segments of a positive life-style, can provide this while also slowing the process of aging. A study performed at the University of Washington some years ago matched 16 young athletes with 11 Masters-age runners (average age 59) of about the same ability. The study found that normal physiological aging is about five percent per decade. Thus, if there are no destructive elements at work on the body, it ages by only 20 percent over 40 chronological years.

Studies of one group of individuals over a 25-year period show that for those who were fairly active, the decline in oxygen consumption was about five milliliters per kilogram of weight. Those who did not exercise lost three times that amount. Rather than observe young athletes with older ones, these and other studies focused on following a specific group of individuals over a quarter century of their lives. The results indicate that the rate of normal decline due to aging may be a bit steeper than previously thought. Thus, some people in the field of exercise physiology are now saying that to truly offset aging may require a higher level of activity than has so far been commonly recommended.

Today, I need only look in the mirror or check my busy activity schedule to see what a higher level of activity did for me.

Psychiatrist Bernice Naughton uses the term *young-old* to describe what she calls a "new aristocracy" of people who are mentally and physically vigorous. We know today that the mind really works better when the body is in motion. The human brain is always awake and its 10 billion cells can either focus on one subject while seeking a problem's solution, or it can switch to automatic pilot and pour out images and thoughts: a stream of consciousness. Philosopher Friedrich Nietzsche once said, "Never trust a thought you came upon while sitting down." And Henry David Thoreau said, "It seems when my legs begin walking my mind begins working."

If exercise is so beneficial, why is it that so many people do little or none? A recent survey by researchers at the Centers for Disease Control in Atlanta, Georgia, found that among the 25,000 adults who were asked if they exercised, only 7.5 percent exercised often enough and hard enough to improve their physical fitness. More than 27.5 percent of the people admitted they did no exercise at all during the two-week period just prior to the interview.

On the other hand, the "more is better" philosophy does not always apply to exercise. I'm referring to those people who do extreme amounts. An article in the February 1988 issue of the newsletter, *Longevity*, suggested that individuals who, for instance, run more than 35 miles a week *may* generate a chemical breakdown in their blood that could have damaging effects.

The fact is, no one yet knows how much exercise is too much.

But we do know what happens when we are prevented from getting exercise. A number of studies have shown that following two weeks of bed rest, a person's pulmonary and cardiac efficiency can be reduced by up to 40 percent, with maximal oxygen uptake down by as much as 20 percent. Medical researchers have established a rule of thumb that one should allow a month of exercise for every year of inactivity. The good news is that this physical decline is reversible and, as Dr. Herbert deVries of the University of Southern California has found, people up to the age of 90 who institute a controlled exercise program can experience remarkable improvement. And the formerly bed-ridden person who gets moving again can raise maximal oxygen uptake by as much as 33 percent.

The American Heart Association (AHA), however, points out that not all kinds of exercise provide the same amount of benefit. What is important is how the cardiovascular system is made to work. Even mild exercise, that prescribed for a person who has suffered a heart attack, can, for example, raise the blood level of those "good fats," the high density lipoproteins. In one study, 32 middle-aged men with coronary artery disease who went on a 13-week exercise program where they walked or jogged an average of 1.75 miles three times a week found that their HDL levels rose.

AEROBIC EXERCISE IS THE KEY

To be effective, exercise should increase the continuous flow of blood through the heart and large muscles. To ensure that *continuous* flow, the exercise has to be one that can be maintained over a period of time—usually at least 20 minutes—three times a week.

We call such exertion "aerobic" and the ideal type supplies a steady amount of oxygen throughout the exercise period. Another way to look at it is that an aerobic exercise is one in which the body is taking in as much oxygen from the air as it is burning to feed the muscles. (In an anaerobic activity, your body burns up more oxygen than it is getting.) Start-stop activity, such as tennis or golf, does not provide the continuous flow of oxygen at the exercise level, nor do strength-building routines such as weight lifting.

Walking at a brisk pace, jogging, and running all provide continuous motion of the legs and, to a lesser degree, move the arms also. As a result, the lung capacity increases and the muscles are made to tense and relax alternately, which aids the flow of blood through them.

Aerobic exercise, to be most effective, should use the muscles of both the arms and the legs, as well as of the large muscle groups in the lower half of the body. The idea is to spread the work load over a wide area. Thus, people with arthritis should exercise not just afflicted parts, but the arms, legs, and torso.

Among the best aerobic activities are bicycling, cross-country skiing (either on actual snow or with indoor machines), brisk walking, swimming, rowing in a boat or with a machine, and dancing. Running is fine if your body is built for that sort of exercise. Those who are not—and even some who are—risk a range of injuries to muscles and bones.

By exercising this way regularly, you will soon find—perhaps to your surprise—that you are able to walk, run, or otherwise move over long distances with little effort, and you will not be breathing hard when you stop. That's because you have developed a comfortable balance between the level of oxygen being carried through your lungs and cardiovascular system and the level your body actually requires for this amount of work. The result is effective aerobic exercise.

THE STRESS TEST

The AHA cautions, however, that before you begin any strenuous exercise program, particularly if you have not exercised for some time, you should ask your doctor to give you a thorough physical check-up that includes a comprehensive evaluation of your cardiovascular system, blood pressure, muscles, and joints. The blood test should include the level of cholesterol and triglycerides (fatty substances) and an electrocardiogram, while both resting and while putting the heart under stress during exercise. The results will tell the doctor how much oxygen you are consuming and how your heart is responding to the exercise. This Stress Test usually involves walking on a treadmill or pedaling on an exercycle, with the degree of work required increased at progressive intervals.

THE HUMAN VEHICLE

Consider the body as an automobile to understand its interrelationships. We think of the human heart as driving the body. On the contrary, the heart is not the engine but more the fuel pump. Indeed, the heart's role is more mechanical than creative. The heart muscle enlarges with activity and increases the organs' output. As a result, efficiency improves and the heart works better.

The lungs are basically a "gas tank" that takes in the "gas" we need—oxygen.

The individual muscle cells are the engines that change chemical energy from what we eat into physical energy. Nine tenths of all our calories are burned by muscles. Moderate exercise, such as a long, brisk walk, burns up excess fat. More intense exercise uses carbohydrates for energy. Carbohydrates are stored in the muscles and liver in glycogen. During exercise, the glycogen is converted to a simple sugar called glucose, which circulates in the blood to be used as needed by muscles and other tissues.[1]

The physically fit person's muscles will use up glycogen more efficiently than those of the "out of shape" individual, and thus can work longer. Protein is used by the muscle cell to make or repair tissue.

Our goal with exercise is to streamline the human vehicle to increase its efficiency—and that of its engine—so that we can go farther on a "gallon of gas." By delivering more oxygen to the heart, its pumping action is improved and the whole cardiovascular system operates more easily.

---

[1] If you exercise so much that all the glucose is used up, the result is hypoglycemia, low blood sugar.

WHY EXERCISE?

Dr. George Sheehan makes an interesting point when he says that the human machine has not been upgraded or improved in recent history. Health and fitness rules have remained the same since Hippocrates practiced medicine about 400 B.C. What is different now is that medical science continues to discover more about how the mechanism works. As you begin your exercise program, follow Dr. Sheehan's four-part formula for effective exercise:

Mode	Involve large muscle groups;
Duration	Maintain at least 30 minutes of continuous movement three to four times a week—and don't count the miles, only the minutes;
Intensity	Increase from fairly light to fairly vigorous exercise, as you "dial your body to 'comfortable' then put it on auto pilot";
Frequency	Aim to exercise every other day, keeping in mind that the two-day rest allows the training effect to take place.

HOW TO EXERCISE SAFELY AND EFFECTIVELY

Almost no exercises are always right or wrong for everybody at all times, because no two people have the same needs or abilities. It is most important that people beginning to exercise be sensitive to their own needs, have definite goals in mind, and be aware of their existing fitness level. Your main concern should be not only following the three-part structure of warm-up, aerobic session, and cool-down, but also to prevent overexertion, contortion, and exhaustion. Thus, while aerobic exercise must be at a high-enough level of activity to condition the heart and muscles, it should not be beyond your safe limit.

Gail Weaver, an exercise physiologist at the University of California, San Diego Extension, and Director of the Good Health Centers and Lifetime Health and Nutrition Centers there, notes that those who want to prevent injury while they work to improve certain parts of their bodies should follow certain rules.

- Warm up properly. The safest way to stretch is to be able to relax while doing it. To prepare for an aerobic exercise session, you must warm up the muscles gently, before you start stretching. You can jog at a slow pace, walk along rapidly, or use an exercycle for at least five minutes. When you begin to feel warm, you are starting to perspire, and your heart rate is up a bit, only then should you go into your stretching exercises. Dress for the weather outside. If it is cold, wear a warm sweat suit; when it is hot, put on shorts. This pre-stretch warm-up raises the temperature of the muscles and tendons and increases their flexibility, while releasing the body's natural joint lubricant, synovial fluid. The heart, too, needs time to warm up or you risk bringing on a dangerous abnormality in the blood flow and blood pressure. Then, after about five minutes of careful stretching, you are ready for the "main event," a healthy workout. Stand correctly. "If you're not in the proper position when you begin the exercise you won't execute the exercise correctly when you begin to move."

- Relax the neck and shoulders. It is common to see new exercisers trying hard and tending to "crunch" their shoulders as they concentrate on body movements. "Contracting shoulder muscles so that the shoulders shrug hurts the neck and puts the shoulder muscles in the wrong position for conditioning."

- Stretch to the side before bending forward. Moving the big muscles that wrap around from your back in the waist area in a side-to-side movement will help prevent back pain or injury.

- Keep nonworking muscles relaxed. Don't tighten up muscles that haven't been called upon to move. Unless they are needed for the particular exercise, try to consciously relax neck, arms, shoulders, back, and knees.

- Move smoothly and continuously. If you jerk suddenly from one position to another without letting your body know ahead of time, you are asking for injury. This once popular, but no longer recommended, ballistic stretching brought on many muscle tears from either overstretching with a "bounce stretch" or from sudden straining or pushing.

- Protect your back and don't forget your knees. If an exercise causes you even a slight strain in these areas, stop.

- If you have back pain, avoid sit-ups with straight legs, flutter kicks while lying flat on your back, and exercises that require you to lie on your side and prop up your torso with one straight arm. Avoid extremes unless you are extremely fit. This includes deep knee bends, double leg lifts from flat on your back, and the yoga "plow" position.

Is Walking Really Enough?

Consider the West Virginia study of women aged 50 to 63 who spent six months walking two miles a day, four days a week. The results were improvement in their cardiovascular and muscle systems comparable to those gained through an aerobic dance program.

So, pick an exercise you enjoy. If you're having fun, you will continue to do it.

WHAT BRINGS FORTH MAXIMUM ENDURANCE LEVEL?

A University of Minnesota School of Public Health study found that endurance capacity appears not to be connected or influenced by blood pressure level, serum cholesterol, alcohol consumption (assuming a maximum of about two drinks per day or 12 per week), irregular heart beat, or sleep habits.

Dr. Sheehan also emphasizes that the physical workout should not be something simply repetitive and boring, a distasteful time you simply endure. If exercise is counting how many times you can do something, sooner or later you will lose interest.

On the other hand, he adds, "Play and sports are the opposite. Play is pure fun. Sport—which is play intensified—is where there are rules, a score, and sometimes a risk. Sport unlocks the enthusiasm and discipline necessary to satisfy our psychological and sociological needs.

Sport thus combines the science that is exercise with the art that is play. In order to keep exercising without becoming bored or disinterested we need to have elements of play and sport. The answer, according to Dr. Sheehan, is to tailor our exercise program to be play, as well as interesting and involved with people. That way, we will be motivated to schedule it as a pleasant part of our regular activities and to continue it week after week.

While Dr. Sheehan promotes any aerobic exercise, at heart he is a runner who becomes rapturous when describing what being in competition does for him. "The race is more than the moment. The subconscious is being purged and rinsed and cleansed; it is being emptied of all the mean and embarrassing things I have accumulated during my life . . . I am replacing all the depressing memories, all the dirt and debris with something that is bright and clean and positive." All this "cleansing" is very necessary, he says, because the subconscious is the source of all our creativity, and creativity—in whatever field or endeavor—rests on a subconscious that has what is "good, true, and joyful." In the midst of people who are quick to find things that are wrong, "the sense of success in the exercise counters this and brings us good feelings about ourselves."

On the physical side, of course, exercise keeps us slim. The traditional view has long been that to reduce body fat means you must reduce food intake. A new view on the matter holds that the body dissipates calories even without movement, possibly through production of heat. It has been found that when an athlete rests, he or she is still using up energy; such cycles may persist for up to three days following the exercise. Aerobic exercise actually causes a hypermetabolic state, so that when the exercise is continued, all the body's functions are set higher, much like turning up a thermostat. As a result, the exerciser can use the same amount of energy at rest that other people do when moving.

Some people believe that dieting alone will take off the weight they want to lose. The problem is that diet by itself reduces not only fat but muscle, and the dieter ends up with a haggard look. True, dieting lets one lose accumulated water, but that is not losing actual mass. Also, loss of muscle means "losing ground," because when the diet is over it is even easier to gain that weight back again on a frame with weakened muscles.

It's Not All Sweetness and Light

Perhaps this is the time to do away with a persistent myth that many runners still believe: Swallowing a sugary drink, or otherwise consuming sugar while exercising, boosts your stamina and holds off fatigue. While it is true that sugar levels can fall during a strenuous workout, as we saw in Chapter Three, sugar will only provide short-term energy, so it may *not* give you the strength to run another mile.

The principal physiological changes that take place during fitness training programs can be measured in two key ways:

- Physical work capacity: the ability to finish a distance (endurance, not speed), which can increase greatly as fitness is developed.

- Oxygen uptake ability: the capacity for an all-out effort, a capability that does not increase more than about 20 percent during training.

Thomas Curtis Namey, M.D., Associate Professor of Medicine and Radiology at the Medical College of Ohio and Chairman of the Board of Examiners of the American Academy of Sports Physicians, points out that what he calls "the breadth of sport today" has broadened the scope of what is now possible in the lives of millions of people, especially those in older age groups. "More and more Masters-level records are being set that are identical if not better than those set by young males 50 to 60 years ago. In fact, a 60-year old today can run a marathon faster than a 20-year old could in 1910."

Dr. Namey sees fitness as the way, if not to lengthen life, at least to make it whole and fulfilling throughout. He echoes Doctors Fries and Crapo in their book *Vitality in Aging* when he says, "Wouldn't it be wonderful if humans could lead a vital and vigorous life, then suddenly become ill and in a very short period of time have a terminal event." The tragedy of modern existence, as he sees it, is that

> We see so many people in our society dying slowly. They may live to be 85, but between 65 and 85 they are three quarters of the way into the grave...There's nothing sadder than a 55-year old person bed-ridden or living in a nursing home. That is *premature functional death*, which is as bad or perhaps worse than premature death.

In short, we're living longer and enjoying it less. Indeed, statistics from the continuing health survey of several hundred thousand people conducted annually by the National Center for Health Statistics in Washington, D.C., indicate that while death rates from heart attack and stroke have declined dramatically in recent years, credited largely to improved treatment of high blood pressure, chronic disease among the middle-aged and older population is on the rise and is becoming more severe. During the 1970s, for instance, the percentage of people aged 45 to 64 who reported a chronic condition serious enough to limit their time on the job rose by about one-third. Among the nonfatal ailments on the rise were arthritis, gout, and upper gastrointestinal disorders.

Dr. Namey concedes that with all the leisure time on hand, and the distractions of a sophisticated society, keeping in shape today is not all that easy. In 1910, people did not have to worry about getting enough physical exercise. They simply had to work many long hours to earn a living. "Today, we have to deal with couch potatoism as a disease."

In fact, he says, physical inactivity itself is a disease. Consider the multi-system consequences it promotes: hypertension, obesity, three times the risk of cardiovascular problems, digestive and bowel problems, and peripheral vascular circulatory problems. All the calcium in the world will not maintain bone calcium until the bone is put under stress by weight-bearing exercise. "This is the single most important factor to test for osteoporosis: We prescribe exercise first, then calcium and/or estrogen and medications."

Dr. Namey mentions the American Medical Association estimate indicating that at least 48 percent of deaths untreatable by contemporary medicine are caused by diseases directly related to life-style which, he says, is now the most important factor in premature death among Americans. He then faults a system that discourages doctors from prescribing exercise.

> Medicare pays a doctor twice as much for a 10-minute sciatic nerve block for a bad back as for doing a careful history and physical examination—which takes a great deal more skill than the technical aspects of that nerve block. Patients want doctors to spend more time with them and to focus on physical activity and life-style, but they [the doctors] are not rewarded for doing this.

EXERCISE HAS MANY BENEFITS

Lowers cholesterol

Exercise lowers the "bad" type of cholesterol, LDL—low-density lipoprotein, and when you burn off 1000 or more calories per week, it increases the "good" cholesterol, HDL—high-density lipoprotein.

Lowers high blood pressure

Although we know that exercise helps a person lose weight, until a few years ago few doctors thought it lowered high blood pressure directly. Now we know that even just exercise alone can bring it down. Exercise does lower blood pressure because it helps the small vessels increase in size, and during exercise the level of two of the body's stress producing hormones, norepinephrine and adrenalin, rises by 300 to 400 percent and the body is actually using up the excess of these hormones stored in nerve endings.

Lowers stress

Indeed, exercise has an especially beneficial effect on stress because it is connected with the "flight-or-fight" response that churns out adrenalin for a person caught in a threatening or merely stressful situation. All that extra adrenalin is fine when coupled with vigorous physical activity, as it was when, for instance, primitive man had to fight a wild beast. Today, when we have largely eliminated the physical activity portion, stress alone can be quite harmful.

Exercise thus reintroduces the element of physical activity, which lets a person's body handle the adrenalin response in a healthy way.

Helps those with diabetes

Diabetics who exercise find that it can lower the amount of insulin they need to take. The exercise helps metabolize glucose, allowing the insulin to work more efficiently.

Helps with weight loss

Exercise also helps with weight problems where dieting alone may not help. When dieting, a person initially loses retained water, then begins to lose fat and muscle. The problem is that as people age, the amount of muscle decreases while fat—because it is an active metabolic tissue—increases.

Through exercise, you not only burn off calories but you also raise your body's metabolic level, which stays high for several hours after the exercise period. As a result, calories continue to burn. In addition, the release of adrenalin during exercise satisfies hunger somewhat. So the more you exercise, the less you may overeat.

Combats depression

Exercise releases beneficial brain chemicals—the endorphins—that have a calming effect and that make you feel good.

MY CURRENT HEALTH PROGRAM

Since age 80, I have changed my exercise program considerably. Not that I was not able to do what I was doing, but from past experience I do not think that running alone gives the body an overall exercise. Now I run three or four miles, three to four times a week. I also use my mini-trampoline each day for 30 to 60 minutes. You must defy gravity when exercising, and every cell in your body does this when you rebound. This exercises every part of the body gently.

I ride my exercise bike for about one hour each day. I do 15 minutes with the light weights (25 pounds) and some floor situps and pushups.

I also do controlled breathing. Think about your breathing. Do some power breathing. You cannot live very long without it.

I go out in the sun every day for ten minutes, in the near nude.

I do a lot of reading and thinking. Thoughts are nothing until you put them into action. As the subconscious mind is our computer, we must program it as to what we want to know and what we want to do. There is nothing you cannot do if you use the proper method.

One thing we must realize is that there are no nutrients in exercise. The more you exercise, the more nutrients are required. We need energy to exercise and nutrients to provide the energy we need. Our food provides us with nutrients, but our conventional way of life does not give us all nutrients needed; therefore we have deficiencies.

Now at age 90 I can remember when I was old at age 70. That is when I had to make a decision. Did I have to throw in the towel, as I did in the boxing ring when I was fighting, when I was getting beaten? I made my decision then. I had reached my three score and ten, but that was no reason I had to quit.

Chapter Six: Exercise

Your body belongs to you, and you make your own destiny. At any age you can become what you want to be.

For six or seven years I tried everything that I had heard of or read about, and I did improve for that time. Then I knew that something else had to be done. At age 78 I was again slowing down.

At that time I was introduced to honeybee pollen. As I knew nothing about it, I conducted considerable research to find out what it was. As I read what benefits it brought to noted athletes and others, I found that this pollen had all the vitamins and minerals that were in the human body. What else would be needed?

I also found out that this pollen was not man-made; it is completely natural. It is mentioned in the Bible in many ways about 68 times. It has been with man since creation. In my travels in the Far East and other countries, I discovered that pollen is used constantly as a food for health.

As soon as I started using honeybee pollen, I knew it was something I needed. By age 80 I was in better physical condition than I had ever been. I ran my first New York City Marathon, 26.2 miles, at age 80, and will run again at age 90, then again at age 100, then maybe . . . ?

With pollen plus other foods, we do not have a deficiency of nutrients, or a deficiency of life. For hundreds of years people have been looking for something that will keep us youthful through our old age. I have found it—fresh honeybee pollen—the Fountain of Youth.

Chapter Seven

NUTRITION— HEALTH DEPENDS ON WHAT YOU EAT OR DO NOT EAT

> *There would have been no need for medicine if sick men had profitted by the same mode of living and regimen as the food, drink, and mode of living of men in health.*
>
> —Hippocrates, 400 B.C.

In the early 1970s, Alexander Leaf, M.D., then Chief of Medical Services at Massachusetts General Hospital and a Professor at Harvard Medical School, visited three places in the world where "time moves kindly." In the region of Abkhazia in the Caucasus Mountains of southern Russia, he found many Georgians well into their 90s and beyond who still worked six days a week, could read without glasses, could hear well, and were disease free. He also noted that the aged Georgians—a number of them were well over 100—consume about 1,800 calories a day, considerably less than the 3000 plus taken in by the average American today. Further, Soviet researchers had determined that the plasma cholesterol level for those over 100 averaged less than half that accepted as normal for Americans aged 50 to 60.

Dr. Leaf and other scientists from the United States also visited residents in the Andean village of Vilcabamba in Ecuador and the Hunza region of Pakistan-controlled Kashmir, where they found similar populations of healthy and long-lived people.

The diet of a sample of adult males in Hunza was found to average 1923 calories a day, which included 354 grams of carbohydrates, 50 grams of protein, and 36 grams of fat. Average American diets at the time had 3300 calories, consisting of 380 grams of carbohydrates, 100 grams of protein, and 157 grams of fat.

At the time of Dr. Leaf's visit to Vilcabamba, there were no doctors or hospitals there, and while most illnesses seemed to heal themselves, those who needed medicine were treated with fasting and herbs. Dr. Leaf found that broken bones were almost non-existent among those people, and that thanks to constant activity their bones were adequately mineralized, dense, and strong. Dr. Leaf later commented that "with inactivity at any age, our bones lose their calcium salts and become thin and fragile."

An internationally known cardiologist, Dr. Miguel Salvador, had visited these people a few years earlier and had tested more than 300 of them. He found no sign of aging in arteries or in circulation and no heart disease in family backgrounds.

So what is their secret of health and long life? The answer appears to be nutritious foods low in fat, lots of exercise, and lack of stress.

Vilcabambians eat slowly and consume small amounts. Their diet is high in carbohydrates, low in protein, and includes little meat.

I hear some readers saying "This is not life-style, but good genes. These people are programmed by their ancestors to have disease-resistant bodies."

Consider another situation: During World War II, many Europeans underwent severe reductions in the amount of fat and protein they consumed in their diets, and their caloric intake fell to about 1,200 to 1,400 a day. Also, because roads and railroads were taken over for military purposes, people often had to walk or ride bicycles. Thus, many people exercised far more than in previous times. The result: a drastic drop in heart trouble and hypertension (high blood pressure).

When peace came to those countries, the citizenry returned to their former habits of overeating and underexercising and—not unexpectedly—soon exhibited a sharp rise in obesity and heart attacks.

For yet another example, consider how the Japanese, whose traditional diet has been low in fat and high in seafoods, have been relatively free of breast and colon cancer. People in rural areas who still eat their traditional diet have good health and good teeth. Their dental decay rate, for instance, is about half that of city dwellers and those who migrate to the United States and begin eating our traditionally high-fat meals. Within 20 to 30 years, the Japanese-Americans display the same levels of breast and colon cancer as those whose families have lived here for many generations.

In China, where rice is the staple diet, it is combined with many other foods and often the mixture is steamed together.

Traditionally, many Chinese laborers lived to be 100 years of age. As modern foods were introduced and the lives of these people became more sedentary, they did not burn up the calories in their rice diet and began to report digestive problems. When the rice was refined, a vitamin B deficiency called beriberi began to occur.

In Mexico, too, the diet of rural dwellers is superior to those who live in the cities. The villagers' diet consists of corn tortillas, beans, rice, cheese, chili peppers, wild greens, fruits and flowers, and a little meat. The tortillas provide ample calcium, which comes from the limestone used in grinding corn and from the fire ash added to the corn meal. Ample sunlight supplies the vitamin D that lets their bodies retain the maximum amount of calcium, producing strong bones and fine teeth.

When the tortillas are eaten with beans, the protein value is equal to that found in meat. Chili peppers provide the final nutritional elements. Beverages include coffee, hot chocolate and pulque, and fermented juice from the maguey (cactus) plant which provides a fine source of vitamin C.

As recently as the 1970s, among Mexico's Otomi Indians living in one of the country's depressed areas, 80 percent of the children and 43 percent of the adults had perfect teeth. The overall figure for perfect teeth in the United States at the time was less than two percent.

My point is that when man first came upon this earth, the land was clean and new and abundant with the fruits that grew there for the benefit of all mankind. It still is today in some remote areas. The Bible says: "And God said, behold, I have given you every herb-bearing seed, which is upon the face of all the earth, and every tree, in which is the fruit of a tree yielding seed; to you it shall be for meat" (Genesis 1:29).

Today, while our bodies are essentially the same as in biblical times, we are consuming the fruits of civilization instead of the fruits of the earth.

Ironically, as it is with exercise, many people still do not pay attention to what they eat. This is despite the rapidly growing mass of research showing that what we eat is often implicated in the diseases with which we are stricken.

More than a decade ago (in 1977), the U.S. Senate Select Committee on Nutrition issued its *Dietary Goals for the United States*. The report proposed that the American diet should have fewer refined and processed sugars, less salt, less cholesterol, less alcohol, fewer calories, but more roughage and more complex carbohydrates—such as potatoes, bread, grain products, vegetables, rice, pasta, and beans—which are broken down slowly in the body so the level of glucose in the bloodstream stays at a proper level for hours.[1]

This type of diet, nutritionists claim, could reduce obesity by 80 percent, heart disease by 25 percent, and produce a 50-percent decline (or improvement) in diabetes cases. Further, they said, there would be a one-percent annual increase in longevity.

The 1984 release of a 10-year study by the National Institutes of Health showed that people who reduced cholesterol levels had a clear reduction in heart disease, this while about

---

[1] Simple "carbos," which break down quickly and cannot be utilized as efficiently as glucose, include white and brown sugar, honey, jam, jelly, candy, sweets, and fruit—although the latter's fiber content slows down digestion and the release of glucose into the bloodstream.

half the Americans in the 45-65 age levels were demonstrating a cholesterol level high enough to cause heart disease.

A report in the *Journal of the National Cancer Institute* found that dietary elements were the largest single category of risks that could be modified, noting that a third of all cancer deaths might be related to diet and that changes in diet could bring a 90-percent reduction in deaths from stomach and bowel cancer, as well as a 50-percent cut in the number of people who die of uterine and breast cancers.

The highly respected British medical journal, *Lancet*, reported in 1985 on research indicating an inverse relationship between the amount of vitamin C and calcium in the diet and the degree of decrease in colon and rectal cancer. Researchers at Memorial Sloan Kettering Cancer Center reported in the *New England Journal of Medicine* that same year that supplementary calcium could reduce abnormal cell activity in the bowel.

Studies noted in the book, *Dr. Berger's Immune Power Diet*, showed that increases in the amount of vitamins C, E, A and B-12, as well as selenium and zinc, strengthen the body's immune system.

Still, the human body remains geared for regeneration. As Robert Rodale states in the *Natural Healing and Nutrition Annual 1988*, the human system is a "pulsing, humming mass of regenerative processes—cells replace cells, tissues heal, muscles expand, nerves and organs change to meet new biological demands." Thus, he adds, "regenerative nutrition is a way of turning up the body's existing regenerative power."

My formula for good health states it more simply: Eat only pure, nutritionally complete foods, and eat very little at any one time.

NEED AN ENERGY RECHARGE? TRY GRAZING

Eat like a cow grazing—nibble on nuts, sip a little yogurt, eat a salad. Stay with small amounts of light and nutritious foods, eating several times a day. This steady but light input of food keeps your blood sugar at a consistent level and your digestive system operating at a steady low level, without the pressure brought by a big meal.

In short, don't load your system with large amounts of protein and carbohydrates. John Pinto, Ph.D., Director of the Nutrition Research Laboratory at Memorial Sloan-Kettering Cancer Center, has pointed out that the secret to gaining the maximum nutrition from what you eat is to consume smaller meals along with nutritional snacks between times. As you "graze," make sure that what you are snacking on contains a balance of protein, carbohydrates, and fiber, plus, of course, vitamins and minerals. Some good choices include: raw fruit and vegetables, yogurt, a hard-boiled egg, perhaps some cheese with dip.

Keep your iron level up with such iron-rich foods as sunflower seeds, raisins, spinach, turkey, and beef liver. Toss in some vitamin C tablets and the body will absorb the iron even better. Also, don't forget to get extra amounts of potassium (in bananas, potatoes, lean meat, oranges, raisins, milk, fish) and magnesium (in whole grain breads, wheat germ, nuts).

Remember, also, that grazing creatures move about slowly while they eat and digest food. So, forget about taking a nap right after eating a meal. Take an easy walk instead.

ABOUT WATER

Drinking water is one of the most important things you can do for your health. Although over two-thirds of our body weight is water, we still need to have a continuing flow of this valuable liquid—six to eight glasses a day. If we don't get enough water, we can become dehydrated and feel sluggish. Also, as we grow older, we lose cellular water—from 10 to 15 percent is gone by age 65. And caffeine, alcohol, sugar, and excess fat all draw water from our cells. This doesn't even include water lost in sweat during exercise or from simple perspiration during a hot day.

Soft drinks and diet sodas are not the answer to lost fluid because they are usually high in caffeine and sodium. By the way, if you are worried about your system retaining too much water, drinking water can help, because it becomes a natural diuretic and flushes out stored water.

ABOUT CHOLESTEROL

This soapy substance, while believed dangerous to our health, is also vital to our body's metabolic needs. Two hundred milligrams per deciliter of blood is considered desirable, up to 240 is "borderline," and above that is "high." Generated daily by our liver, cholesterol is a key ingredient in shaping cell members, making bile to help digestion of fat, and manufacturing sex and stress hormones. Unfortunately, too much cholesterol brings a high risk of coronary heart attack. The American Heart Association recommends that to keep cholesterol under control involves seeking a life-style that keeps weight down, includes exercise, and excludes saturated fats.

Among recent scientific findings in the battle to lower cholesterol is that monounsaturates such as olive and peanut oil, previously considered neutral in the matter, may be strong warriors against cholesterol. Researcher Scott M. Grundy, M.D., Ph.D., Director of the Center for Human Nutrition of the University of Texas Health Science Center in Dallas, found (as reported in the *New England Journal of Medicine*, March 11, 1986) that such oils lowered both overall cholesterol and, more importantly, the dangerous low-density lipoprotein (LDL). These results coincide nicely with observations that the rate of cardiovascular disease in areas where people cook with olive oil—the Mediterranean, in particular—is quite low.

There is some good news on the cholesterol front. Dr. Grundy of the University of Texas reports that during the past 20 years, average cholesterol levels have decreased from 230 to 210 and the United States no longer leads the world in high coronary heart attack rates. That dubious honor now belongs to some European nations whose citizens still have not taken to heart advice on how to reduce cholesterol intake.

Moreover, it now appears that not all saturated fats are bad. A preliminary study in Boston, reported in the *New England Journal of Medicine* in May 1988, indicates that one type of fat found in beef and other foods seems to lower cholesterol in the manner of polyunsaturated and monounsaturated fats. This study is, as noted, preliminary, and the researcher, Dr. Grundy, who is also Past Chairman of the American Heart Association's Nutrition Committee, suggests that "beef eaters" limit themselves to three-ounce portions of select-grade meat and, as the AHA recommends, restrict fat intake to 30 percent of total calories, with not more than a third of that amount in saturated fat.

DIETING CAN BE HARMFUL TO YOUR HEALTH

Obesity—defined as being 20 percent or more over your ideal weight—is usually attributed to overeating, especially fat and carbohydrates, combined with underexercise. However, undereating in this case is not the answer and some researchers have claimed for years that those who diet may instead gain weight.

Janet Polivy, Professor of Psychology and Psychiatry at the University of Toronto General Hospital, cautions that overweight people must start by accepting themselves as they are and not think of weight loss and improved appearance as a magic solution. Otherwise, she declares, they may become involved in strict diets that promise rapid weight loss only to end up going on an eating binge because they have been deprived of the foods they really need or want.

Two books published in 1988 stress that strict dieting can be counterproductive or even damaging to your health.

In *Overcoming Overeating,* New York psychotherapists Jane Hirschmann and Carol Hunter stress that overweight people should look to other benefits in a diet, even if they don't lose weight. In other words, people should stop criticizing themselves for being fat, be more positive about their self-image, and be able to eat what they need when they need it.

Psychobiolgist Dale M. Atrens, a Professor at the University of Sydney, Australia, argues in *Don't Diet* that people can be healthy even if they are overweight—if they exercise and eat foods low in fats and high in carbohydrates. Dieting, on the other hand, carries with it the risk of developing eating disorders.

Indeed, there is research to show that when people go on strict diets their bodies may see the strict regime as a threat and rebel by slowing down the metabolic processes. The result is no more weight loss. In addition, some obesity may not be due to overeating at all. One researcher has estimated that only 20 percent of overweight people overeat.

Good advice for chronic dieters seems to be to have a plan that reduces weight gradually in order to return the rate at which the body burns food (the metabolic rate) to normal. According to at least one estimate, such a regimen should allow *at least* 10 calories per pound of weight per day. Thus, a 150-pound person must have at least 1,500 calories.

The *New Complete Medical Encyclopedia, Volume Three,* 1987, notes that a fairly accurate method for an adult to calculate daily caloric need is to take his or her desirable weight for given height and frame sizes and multiply by 18 for a man, 16 for a woman. (If your day includes strenuous or vigorous exercise, more calories will be needed.)

The total number of calories in your diet should, ideally, be distributed in the following quantities:

- 50 to 60 percent from carbohydrates (mostly from complex carbohydrates, such as vegetables and whole grains),
- 15 percent from protein, and
- 25 to 30 percent from fats.

FOODS THAT SHORTCHANGE YOU OF NUTRIENTS

Food serves three basic functions in the body: It provides material to be metabolized into energy; it supplies electron donors (electrochemical particles) that allow the necessary enzymes to be formed to drive the processes within each cell; and it provides the elements to build new living cells.

What constitutes bad foods?

Let's start with hydrogenated vegetable oil. "Hydrogenated" means hydrogen has been added. Untreated oils contain substances known as antioxidants that prevent the oil from turning rancid. These antioxidants also prevent destruction of fat-soluble vitamins (A, D, E, K, and several of the Bs, plus carotene), both in the food and in the body's intestinal tract. When hydrogen is added to the oils, it lowers the antioxidant level and serious amounts of the vitamins are lost from the food before they reach the bloodstream.

Try to avoid refined and processed foods. They, too, are not only changed chemically to where they lose much of their nutrients but they may actually be harmful. For instance, rancid oil is thought to cause certain malignancies, and some fast-food restaurants have been known to keep french-fry oil for days. Also, french fries themselves are made from partially precooked potatoes—nutritionally "dead food."

Finally, the refined carbohydrates (sugars) in many brands of cookies, doughnuts, pies, and other pastries reach the digestive tract with most of the real nutrients missing.

GETTING THOSE MISSING NUTRIENTS

How do we ensure that we get the essential nutrients?

Researchers at the University of California, San Diego, Medical Center's Clinical Research Center have listed 10 of the healthiest foods for the future. All have high nutrient-to-calorie ratios and thus more food value per calorie. They are:

non-fat yogurt;

tofu—a soybean product;

amaranth—a high protein grain;

oat bran—its highly soluble fiber cuts cholesterol and controls blood sugar;

broccoli, cauliflower, and other members of the cabbage family, high in A, C, calcium and fiber;

vegetable pastas—less fat and more fiber than regular pastas;

range-fed lean meats—in small amounts, a fine source of iron and zinc;

seafood—shrimp, clams, crab, lobster, oysters, salmon, tuna (low in calories and saturated fat, high in unsaturated fat);

sorbets or fruit ices—concentrated natural fruit juices, fiber, virtually no fat;

and **popcorn**—low in fat, calories, high in fiber.

Brown rice, buckwheat, barley, corn, millet, and wheat—we think of these foods as valuable for their fiber content. Indeed, they are also free of cholesterol, low in fat, and high in the B vitamins and vitamin E, plus protein, iron, magnesium, and selenium. Thus, by increasing your consumption of grain, while lowering the amount of whole-fat dairy foods, you can achieve the low-fat, high-fiber diet now seen as the way to prevent many diseases.

Finally, fresh honeybee pollen is a nutritionally complete and physically rejuvenating dietary supplement.

Noel makes a strong finish after a full day of cold, driving rain. New York City Marathon.

Chapter Eight

HONEYBEE POLLEN— THE NUTRITIONAL MIRACLE

Pollen the beautiful is the force within us.

—Navajo Medicine Man

Many people wake up their bodies (and minds) in the morning with a cup of coffee. I prefer to wake up by refueling myself with crucial nutrients in a compact form. Thus, my first act upon arising is to take a couple of tablets of fresh honeybee pollen.

As one writer has noted, "Pollen in plants is what sperm is to animals—the agent of viability."

To me, it is simply the stuff of life.

Pollination is fertilization, and humans have practiced it for a long time. The ancient Assyrians are reported to have hand-pollinated date palms. Carved slabs of stone found in the palace of Ashuir-nasir-pal II—who ruled the Assyrian empire from 885 to 860 B.C.—and now exhibited in New York's

Metropolitan Museum of Art, depict a symbolic male figure placing seeds in the fruit on a tree.

Pollinating by hand generally was no easy task, due mostly to the size of pollen grains. The largest are barely visible to the naked eye, and someone has figured out that one could put 10,000 of the smallest—from a forget-me-not plant—on the head of a pin. These tiny bits of life, some less than 1/700th of an inch in diameter, could not even be seen until the invention of the microscope in the mid-17th century. The first person to describe pollen kernels was an English physician named Nehemiah Grew in a book entitled *Anatomy of Plants* (published in London in 1682).

Dr. Grew found that the mostly yellow particles resemble dust or meal—the word pollen comes from the Latin "fine flour"—and are usually spherical in shape. When magnified 3000 times they reminded him of Holland cheese, tiny peppercorns, or even fish. Others have described the enlarged images as being like organic Christmas tree bulbs.

While Dr. Grew told us what pollen looks like, it was not until more than a hundred years later, in 1793, that a German scientist named C. K. Sprengel described the process of pollination.

The bees forage among the blossoms, searching for nectar and pollen, which is the principal protein required to form larvae. The pollen granules are on the tip of the pollen tube (or stamen), the male sex organ. As the bees pass by, pollen sticks to the thick bristly hairs on their hind legs and is then scraped off into a "basket" formed between these legs. As the bees flit from flower to flower, some of the pollen is left on the female plant's stigma. If the pollen is from the same species, the host plant recognizes this and the grain is able to unite with the egg in the ovule and form an embryo that then becomes a seed.

When the worker bee has its "basket" filled, it's home to the hive to store the pollen in comb cells.

This is where we humans harvest some of it to add life to our own body's cells. Beekeepers place screens at the entrance to each hive. As the bees pass through on their way to the colony, the screen gently removes much of the pollen, which then drops into a drawer or trap below. The screens are carefully designed so that the bee keeps enough pollen to feed the larvae. The drawer is emptied regularly and the precious pollen is on its way to feed humans.

In certain cultures, notably among some American Indian tribes in hot, arid regions, bee pollen has an almost spiritual significance. The Navajo, in Arizona and New Mexico, for instance, are said to consider pollen a symbol of the core of their existence. To them it represents life itself, and its most valuable aspects: fertility, peace, and power. A medicine man was quoted as saying, "Pollen the beautiful is the force within us."

Does pollen really have powerful benefits for all humans?

I agree with Olympic sprinter Steve Riddick, twice a gold medal winner in the 1976 games, and world-class marathoner Gary Fanelli. As do these two champions, I chew a few extra pollen tablets before starting a race, and I swallow one every so often along the route. I also eat a few spoonfuls of the granules. There are also candy bars made from pollen and honey. Former President Ronald Reagan enjoys these as a part of his personal fitness regimen.

Finland's Olympic coach Seppo Nauuttila put his track team on pollen supplements in the 1970s, and saw them capture four gold medals. Recently, he shifted over to coaching his country's rowing team and still recommends pollen as a nutritional supplement, especially for B vitamins.

In 1982, the Swedish Sports Federation produced a study on the positive effects on human physical endurance and performance of proteins, minerals, vitamins, and—among health foods—pollen.

Researchers A. Bruce, B. Ekblom, and I. Nillson commented that "a number of studies have indicated that because extracts of microbiologically fermented pollen made into tablets contain hydrolyzed proteins, vitamins, minerals, steroids, sugars, and perhaps an as-yet-unidentified pharmacologically active substance; it is food that can cure deficiencies in many of these areas."

Well, that mystery substance may not yet have been uncovered, but what has been learned is reason enough to want to take advantage of the nutritional aspects of honeybee pollen.

In *Pollen: Development and Physiology*, edited by J. Heslop-Harrison (Appleton-Century-Crofts, New York, 1971), Robert G. Stanley of the Forest Physiology Laboratory, University of Florida, notes that although the chemical constituents do vary with the species and the environment, the protein content in pollen is as high as 30 percent of dry weight. Protein values between 5.9 and 28.3 percent were reported. Among the minerals, sulphur and phosphorous are five to ten times as high in pollen as in leaves and roots. Overall mineral content in pollen from, for instance, date palms, is unusually high. Iron and zinc are the most abundant trace elements, along with boron.

Stanley's analysis showed that all the essential amino acids are present in bee pollen and that the total free amino acids and amides are usually higher in pollen than in leaves and other plant tissue. Bee pollen also has all the Krebs Cycle acids as well as fatty acids.

Angiosperm honeybee pollen (pollen from trees whose seeds are enclosed in their own containers—such as apple, almond, and oak) is higher in sugars than that carried to the plants by the wind. Pine pollen, on the other hand, not only has many soluble sugars but enzymes to metabolize absorbed sugars from external sources.

Bee pollen has an ascorbic acid content from 7 mg/g to 15 mg/g, and total vitamin C content is several times higher than this. Stanley comments that this high content of ascorbic acid suggests that honeybee pollen is a source of therapeutic benefit for both humans and animals.

Such pollen has also been found to be very high in carotenes, which behave chemically as enzyme cofactors and have been observed as fulfilling the role of vitamins, a precious precursor in bee nutrition, and considered essential for insects and humans.

By 1974, Stanley, in collaboration with H. F. Linskens, published *Pollen Biology, Biochemistry Management*. Among their findings: The average value of vitamin E in honeybee pollen is 320 mg/gm of pollen fat; riboflavin (B-2) occurs in most bee pollens; and folic acid was found to be higher (up to 6.8 percent of mg/gm dry weight) in pollen carried by honeybees than in that carried by the wind.

All 15 species of honeybee pollen analyzed contained linoleic acid, plus up to eight other fatty acids.

The authors observed that most pollens contain up to seven different steroids—substances related to hormones in humans—and that, "Interestingly, the male sex-organ-inducing sterol antheridiol produced by the male mycelium of Achylya bisexualis can be derived from sterols common to pollen." They added that tests suggest that at least three male hormones may be present as glucuronides.

They also concluded that pollen is endowed with a considerable range of enzymes, and the capacity to form or activate many enzymes during growth.

THOSE ENZYMES WORK

I have now been taking fresh honeybee pollen for more than a decade to refuel my body and to keep me in top physical condition. The longer that I continue to use bee pollen in my daily life, the more convinced I become that it will be a vital ingredient of future foods throughout the world to maintain health and promote longevity.

Fresh honeybee pollen is a fundamental element of my personal rejuvenation program. I credit this incredible storehouse of vitamins, minerals, hormones, amino acids, enzymes, and coenzymes with helping me back to full vigor, restoring my manhood, and continuing to protect my health by nourishing every cell. The honeybee pollen's extraordinary richness gives me the energy I need to run in marathons and to do all the other activities that require physical stamina far, far beyond that typical of a person my age.

I have no doubt that Mother Nature's bee pollen must be the perfect food in today's world. It is a pure vegetable product that I believe contains more amino acids than meat, cheese, or eggs.

With vaccines and other medicine, we conquered the major infectious diseases of the 19th century, such as tuberculosis, diphtheria, and smallpox. Today's scourges of mankind are, as we already know, degenerative afflictions such as heart attacks, cancer, emphysema, osteoporosis, and degenerating joint problems. These are, as we indicated in Chapter Seven, to a large extent within our ability to prevent. Much has to do with how we treat our bodies and how we keep them supplied with the basic nutrients they need to be in top health and condition. I'm totally convinced that bee pollen supplies your body with *all* the nutrients needed to maintain vitality, energy, and, yes, also youth.

Sadly, for us in America, much of the most definitive research done to date on bee pollen has been done in Europe and has not received the proper notice in this country that it deserves.

One program, however, a two-year research project by former Russian Olympic track coach Remi Korchemmy at the Pratt Institute in New York City studied the ability of athletes to recover endurance and stamina. Korchemmy found that athletes who took honeybee pollen not only recovered energy more rapidly than other competitors, but they were even able to improve their performance during second and sometimes third efforts.

It has also been reported that Irving Glick, M.D., team physician for the world champion New York Apples tennis team found success with both professional and amateur athletes who took honeybee pollen on a regular basis.

As I travel about the world lecturing on health and fitness, I'm frequently asked some basic questions about my use of honeybee pollen.

The answers here may prove helpful to readers.

Q. Why haven't we heard much about the benefits that bee pollen has to offer?

A. The benefits through regular use of bee pollen are known quite well in many other countries, where it is used extensively. Traditionally, the medical community in America has been more concerned with curing symptoms rather than preventing disease. Maybe if people started looking at what keeps a human body healthy instead of what makes it sick, we would have more knowledge about the benefits of total nutrition, and thus about the powers of a bee pollen supplement.

Q. How do you eat honeybee pollen?

A. I eat both the granules and the tablets, which I carry with me to munch on during the day, especially when I am traveling.

Q. What is the best way to start eating honeybee pollen?

A. Put one or two granules, or one quarter of a tablet, under your tongue. Let it dissolve and you will find out how your body reacts to it. Some people are allergic to certain substances, such an penicillin or strawberries, for instance. Chances are you won't have a reaction to honeybee pollen. Those people who are allergic to pollen usually find it is the light wind-borne variety, not the heavier type carried by the bees, that they cannot eat. However, this small test will tell you and you won't suffer for it. The following day, eat a little, the next day some more, and you will soon know what amount is best for you.

Q. Can I have an adverse reaction to the use of bee pollen?

A. Some people who are allergic to the pollen of certain plants can get a reaction, which indicates a sensitivity to the chemical changes that pollen makes in your body. Thus, by beginning slowly and building your daily intake gradually you allow your body a chance to overcome any such reaction. Symptoms can range from watery or itchy eyes, flushing, or even slight nausea and gas pains to an asthma attack or, in a very small number of cases, difficult breathing. If you suffer from allergies, see your doctor before you start taking honeybee pollen.

Q. How will I know if I'm taking the right amount?

A. In my opinion, the right amount depends on how physically active you are. I run six to ten miles a day when I train for marathons, so chances are I need more than most others need. But research has shown that one or two 130 mg tablets a day can produce positive results. The best answer, I believe, is to listen to your body and judge for yourself.

Q. When will I start feeling the effects of taking honeybee pollen?

A. People have reported that the first changes they noted were more energy and a feeling of well being, along with needing less sleep. Many noted an improvement of digestion in a week or so. The use of bee pollen has a cumulative effect and so you need to take it for a period of time.

At this time, I am working with Britic (USA), Inc., to devise a program package that will introduce an individual gradually to the healthful benefits of honeybee pollen. The concept behind this program package is to provide initially a small dose of the bee pollen, in tablet form, with an increase in the dosage over a period of weeks. The varying doses will be color coded according to the dose level. In this manner, the dose level can be monitored easily and a routine toward improved health can be established quickly. This bee pollen *program pack* will be a highly researched and developed health food product, unlike any other available in the market.

New York City Marathon trophy and medal.

Chapter Nine

BREATHING RIGHT FOR HEALTH

A breath can make them, as a breath has made.
—Oliver Goldsmith, 1728–1774

HOW BREATHING WORKS

Breathing is defined as the exchange of gases between the atmosphere and the blood. This is accomplished by two human body systems: the respiratory (the lungs, nose, throat, vocal cords, windpipe, and bronchi) and the cardiovascular (the heart, blood, and blood vessels).

More specifically, it is the process that first brings oxygen into the lungs to be transferred to the bloodstream and delivered to the cells, then powers used material out of the body.

The procedure has three distinct segments: we inhale, exhale, and pause. The length of the pause varies during the day and—as the soft drink slogan used to say—it is the "pause that refreshes," because it gives the system a brief recovery time before the next inhalation.

Our bodies are composed of, among other things, masses of tiny blood vessels, called capillaries. Some are as small as four-thousands of an inch in diameter, forcing red blood cells to travel through these tubes in single file. Incoming oxygen stored in the thousands of alveoli (air) sacs in the lungs passes through the capillary walls to meet the blood flowing there.

Once in the blood, the oxygen lets us burn the fuel in the food we eat, thus providing the energy we need to live and to function in life. The quality of the air-oxygen mixture we breathe can influence so many parts of our lives: our stamina and our ability to grow and to function, to heal, to repair damaged areas and to fight off illness. It also affects how fast we age, how we look, how we perceive things, as well as how well we can concentrate or reason.

THE JOURNEY TO THE LUNGS AND BACK

To do all these things, the molecules of oxygen must enter the mouth or through the nostrils, flow past the central divider (the septum), pass by the tonsils (or where they once were), and travel on down the throat (pharynx) by way of the voice box (larynx), and through the wind pipe (trachea) to the lungs.

Just behind the root of the tongue, the oxygen molecules encounter the epiglottis, the "trapdoor" that falls down to block the windpipe when food is on its way to the stomach. The windpipe is actually a tube about four and one-half inches long and roughly three-quarters of an inch in diameter that consists of stacked rings of cartilage covered with a fibrous membrane and lined with a mucous membrane.

The molecule's trip down the trachea delivers it to the bronchi, a structure of tubes resembling an upside-down tree trunk and branches, with two main limbs, the bronchus, one extending into each lung. Within the lung, each bronchus subdivides into smaller tubes called bronchioles, which finally become the tiny twigs that lead to the microscopic, cup-shaped air sacs (alveoli) that line the lung's interior walls. As the incoming air fills the lungs, oxygen is diffused from the alveoli through the membranes of the capillaries and into the blood, then through the interstitial fluid and into the cells. Carbon dioxide goes through the same steps, but in the reverse order: cell to fluid to blood to alveoli sac, and finally on its way back up the route to the outside world.

Other refuse carried to the lungs is ejected by a different process. The bronchi tree exudes a mucous that traps any debris making its way into the lungs. The mucous is then propelled upward by a constant sweeping motion of millions of tiny hairlike cilia.

If there is too much debris or secretion for the cilia to handle, a cough is triggered, serving as the body's built-in system for getting rid of waste in the lungs.

OUR LUNGS

These two cone-shaped organs, separated by the heart, are not equal in size. The right one is about two ounces heavier than the left one and has three lobes to the two of its partner. The lobes have been described as large folds with sizable fissures in between.

They are enclosed by two layers of skin called pleural membranes. A fluid between the two layers keeps the surfaces from rubbing against each other as the lungs expand and contract during breathing. (When these membranes become inflamed and scuff painfully against one another, the result is called pleurisy.)

The average pair of lungs contains an estimated 300 million alveoli, which constitute a surface area of 753 square feet, all crinkled up inside the chest wall.

The lungs are at work constantly, moving air in and carbon dioxide out about 22,000 times a day. Estimates claim that a healthy adult breathes in about 500 gallons of air every 24 hours, inhaling almost a quart of air (from 300 to 400 cubic centimeters) at a time.

A healthy adult averages 12 respirations (the inhale-exhale process) a minute while at rest, taking in an average of 6,000 ml (500 ml with each inhalation). With a very deep breath, a person can pull in as much as 3,500 ml of air.

The accepted method for determining breathing disorders such as bronchitis, asthma, and emphysema is to measure the volume of air entering and leaving the lungs. In the case of emphysema, the alveoli lose elasticity and cannot snap back after air is exhaled. Thus they can't push out the normal amount of air.

Pulmonary infections can cause inflammations that allow fluid to accumulate in the lung air spaces (a condition referred to in Chapter Three), thereby reducing the space available for air and decreasing vital capacity.

While the lungs are the nucleus of the respiratory system, the body parts that fit around it and fuel it are also crucial to effective operation.

The "house" that protects the system includes the ribs, which are able to expand and contract because they are attached to the spine in the back and to the sternum (breastbone) in front by cartilage rather than bone. The ribs are connected to one another by muscles set in an almost crisscross position. The so-called shoulder girdle—also designed to move freely—is the set of bones and tendons that include the clavicle (collar bone) on either side in front and the two scapula (shoulder blades) in the back.

Most of the work of breathing is normally handled not by the lungs but by the diaphragm, a dome-shaped muscle between the bottom of the chest area and the stomach. The diaphragm operates somewhat like a piston. It moves down to contract and pull air in, then releases and the recoil action lets it arch up and force the exhalation, which sends the carbon dioxide up out of the lungs. All this is a rather simple muscle action. But, as with any muscles, it takes oxygen to provide the energy to make it work.

So, oxygen is brought in and carbon dioxide is pushed out. If the carbon dioxide is not eliminated quickly and efficiently, it produces acid, which can be poisonous to the body's cells. It takes the combined efforts of the body's cardiovascular and respiratory systems, working together, to supply the oxygen, remove the carbon dioxide from the cells and maintain the proper acid-to-alkali balance.

THE SPIROMETER

Even healthy individuals with normal breathing capacity may find it is declining as a result of the contaminated air they are forced to breathe. Breathing capacity—how much oxygen you are able to inhale—is also dragged down by disease, and thus is a key indicator of your overall health. Doctors determine that capacity with a simple device called a spirometer.

The importance of this test, which measures the depth of your breathing and in particular the volume of air you exhale, has been demonstrated repeatedly. One of the most well-known applications involves the long-term (almost 40 years) health analysis of a group of citizens in Framingham, Massachusetts. Every two years, the several thousand participants are asked to take the deepest breath they can manage, then expel the air into a tube as rapidly and with as much force as possible.

The resulting volume of air that is exhaled is called the forced vital capacity and is a telltale sign of as-yet-undetected heart or lung disease. If the breathing capacity, as shown by the test, is low, the person has a far greater-than-average chance of an early death—four to six times that of those with high breathing capacities.

The Framingham researchers also found that the lungs' forced vital capacity was an important clue to the rate of *all* cardiovascular diseases and—because it could predict heart failure before any other symptoms appeared—a strong marker for life expectancy. With people who do not have heart disease, yet register low on vital capacity, the test may be detecting lung disease from smoking early enough to take corrective action.

In the average healthy individual, forced vital capacity declines about five percent per decade of life. Among those who smoke, it drops faster. Conversely, among those who exercise, it may erode more slowly.

THE DIFFERENCE IN AIR PRESSURE

Breathing can take place for the same reason that blood flows through the body: a difference of pressure. That is, we breathe in (inhale) when the pressure inside the lungs is less than the atmospheric pressure outside. We breath out (exhale) when the pressure in the lungs exceeds that in the atmosphere.

At the precise instant when we start to exhale, the pressure inside the lungs is identical to that in the atmosphere, 760 millimeters of mercury at sea level. By increasing the volume (expanding) of the lungs while the amount of gas remains the same, the pressure inside becomes less than that outside and air flows in.

Exhaling requires the reverse process—making the lungs smaller to increase the pressure and force the carbon dioxide out into the atmosphere. While inhaling requires the muscles between the ribs to stretch, exhaling is a passive process whereby these muscles relax, the ribs move downward as the diaphragm also relaxes, and its dome moves upward. The alveoli, now empty of air, start to collapse on themselves like the walls of a deflated balloon.

THE HEART OF THE MATTER

How is the heart related to the way we breathe? If the heart is not pumping as well as it should, blood will tend to back up in the millions of capillaries, so they become stiff and swollen with fluid and less able to expand and contract. Also, as fluid builds up around the lungs' cells it is more difficult for incoming oxygen to reach the blood. The result is a gasping for breath.

Some people achieve excellent results on the vital capacity measurement but still end up short of breath and breathing too hard too soon.

The reason for this is clear: They need more exercise. In fact, healthy lungs can handle vast amounts of air, process as much oxygen as the body can hold into the bloodstream, and keep up with virtually any level of physical activity.

Why, then, do people huff and puff? First of all, the blood needs to carry enough oxygen, which means having enough red blood cells and hemoglobin, the substance inside the cells that actually carries the oxygen.If you are short in these areas, the problem may be anemia, usually from not having enough iron, which is critical to healthy hemoglobin and lets it carry the oxygen through the bloodstream.

Or, perhaps the heart cannot pump enough blood. A heart trained with aerobic exercise becomes more muscular and can push along more of the precious liquid with each beat. If the heart has not been strengthened by aerobic exercise, it must beat more often to transfer the same amount of blood. Faster beating is not only less efficient, but it puts more strain on the heart itself.

While the lungs are providing plenty of oxygen, exercise stimulates development of good capillary channels to the muscle tissues, builds up the number and size of the mitochondria (the organelles that play a central role in the production of energy), and increases the substance in the muscles that takes oxygen from the bloodstream into the cells.

If we are short on oxygen, our thinking processes suffer. That's because our brain, while it makes up only about two percent of body weight, uses about 20 percent of our oxygen during complete rest, and even more during physical and mental activity.

Still, most of us are normally not even aware of our breathing. This miraculous process usually happens entirely without our thinking about it. Some people must think about it, though. Singers and actors, for instance, master breath control to gain an effortless flow of oxygen and to be able to sustain a high note or a long dramatic monologue.

During periods of stress or exercise, we automatically breathe more deeply. While asleep, on the other hand, our breathing is more shallow.

There are even times during sleep when some people stop breathing; this is called apnea. Such pauses, even if only for a few seconds, can be dangerous and potentially life-threatening. Fortunately, some little warning signal usually sounds in time and the person wakes with a start, perhaps coughs, and then goes back to sleep.

WORKING TOWARD EFFORTLESS BREATHING

The goal, whether we are awake or asleep, is to have effortless deep breathing. But often that, too, takes a bit of effort.

The religions of ancient Oriental and Near Eastern cultures often stress breath control. For instance, the Taoists of China, who believe in living a life of simplicity and selflessness, stress breath control as a way to live a longer life.

In order to focus body energies and keep the circulatory system healthy, the followers of this faith, whose philosophy dates to the 6th century B.C., would practice something called the Tao Yin, a procedure combining breathing practice with stretching. Taoist teachers taught a technique that consisted of holding in a breath and mentally conducting it through the body. The process was called "feeding on air."

Taoists maintain that breathing is a self-regulating process that lets us automatically return to the normal flow from a period of stress or disturbance. We in the West let adrenalin continue to flow and thus don't let our natural rhythms take over, so we continue abnormal breathing longer than necessary. As a result, we do not gain the advantage of full and deep breathing that can bring back energy and vitality.

The article by Phil Nuernberger, Ph.D., whom we mentioned in Chapter Five, in the October 1985 issue of *Elle* is entitled, "Tap into Your Resources and Go." Among the ideas he discusses is a short exercise designed to let one take a short break one or more times a day and get back to natural rhythms of breathing through "Breath Awareness."

> Choose a quiet spot and sit in an erect but relaxed posture. Don't slouch, as this will interfere with your breathing.
>
> Close your eyes and focus your attention on feeling your breath as it passes in and out of your nostrils. You will sense at the tip of your nostrils a slight coolness as you exhale. If at first you don't feel the coolness or warmth, don't worry—it is important not to analyze or think about what you're doing and instead focus on the physical sensation of breathing.
>
> You will immediately notice three related events: your mind is cleared of thoughts; your breathing becomes smooth and even; and there is a slight release of tension in your body. The longer you maintain this concentration, the greater the mental clarity and relaxation you will experience.
>
> After a few moments of this exercise, imagine that you are drawing each breath to the center of yourself. Think of your body as a shell around you and concentrate on the breaths flowing in and out of this shell.

Practice breath awareness until you can "switch on" without realizing it.

BREATHING WHILE YOU MOVE

Breathing during exercise is a different matter. Bryant Stamford, Ph.D., Director of the Exercise Physiology Department at the University of Louisville's School of Medicine, stresses that "rapid, shallow breathing is extremely unproductive, because you end up moving air back and forth in the 'dead space' between your nose and mouth and the depths of your lungs where oxygen uptake occurs. No oxygen is absorbed from air in the dead space."

Breathe deeply, but not in an unnatural way, he advises, cautioning us not to hold our breaths while exercising—especially if lifting weights—for that can increase blood pressure.

Breathing, while it is the most important factor in our lives, may also be sadly neglected in a number of ways. Our bodies depend on breathing to get rid of gaseous waste from the cells' processes, to expel debris, toxins, and excessive inner heat, as well as to keep the routine metabolic functions in balance and functioning well.

Healthy breathing, which brings in plenty of fresh oxygen and which should be done as much as possible toward the diaphragm, has been credited with providing a long list of benefits. When combined with biofeedback training, it can be an effective way to relax tense muscles. It may also soothe the nerves and ease any physical tensions, decrease carbon dioxide in the blood (thus reducing the acid toxicity that when in excess can be fatal), improve eyesight, and clear the mental processes to let us think more quickly.

Healthy breathing also increases flexibility of ligaments, muscles, and tendons, ensures a well-functioning heart, prevents indigestion and constipation, encourages correct waste elimination through skin pores, increases the health of the liver and kidneys (thus decreasing high blood pressure), and helps lower shortness of breath and "change-of-life" hot flashes.

THE COMMAND CENTER

Finally, there is the body's nervous system. It tells the breathing organs when and how to function. Actually, we all have two nervous systems: The first is the central nervous system, which includes the brain and spinal cord, while the less well- known involuntary nervous system is actually two systems—the sympathetic nervous system and the parasympathetic nervous system.

The sympathetic system is literally in sympathy with what is going on in the body, so it stands ready to set off the fight-or-flight response if a person is in danger. Its opposite, the parasympathetic, helps us rest and repair, in conjunction with the functions of normal daily living such as digestion, perspiration, excretion, and reproduction.

With the sympathetic system in command, breathing becomes heavier, the heart rate and blood pressure go up, and blood leaves the limbs and other outer areas to be able to protect the all-important central organs. Sugar from the liver is rushed to the bloodstream and the digestive system all but stops processing food. In short, the body is geared to do battle against a life-threatening danger.

When the parasympathetic system takes over again, breathing slows down, the heart rate declines, the stomach and the intestinal system go back to work, and things generally get back to a normal and calm state. These systems work automatically, virtually without our being aware of them, or almost automatically.

In recent years, western technology has developed biofeedback devices (described more fully in the next chapter) through which a person can manipulate many of the "automatic" functions such as heart rate, constriction or dilation of blood vessels, and much more.

Biofeedback training now allows a person to learn how to alter bodily systems in various ways. Thus, we are learning to control some of our body's more basic physical processes. In the next chapter, we will take on the mental ones, as we explore that endlessly intriguing master control center for our body: the mind.

Between running and lecturing engagements in Osaka, Japan.

Chapter Ten

YOUR MIND POWER IS THE KEY TO UNLOCKING A HEALTHY LIFE

> *Curiosity is one of the permanent and certain characteristics of a vigorous mind.*
>
> —Samuel Johnson, 1709–1784

The part of our being that allows us to learn is our mind. But that marvelous creation does far more. It not only thinks and is our own individual computer, but it maintains awareness through our five senses, feels through our emotions, records into memory, and controls our actions.

Like most people, I always assumed that my mind must be located in my brain. Yet, despite detailed dissection and study of the three-pound, softball-sized spongy mass of nerve cells we call the human brain, no one has been able to see or otherwise locate this elusive "seat of the intellect."

It seems we may never find it and perhaps we finally have an idea why. Some neuroscientists and others who have given the mystery a lot of thought now believe that the mind is not a *thing* at all but a *process* that occurs in the brain and nervous system.

It is this process that can be a powerful tool in slowing the aging process. Unfortunately, many people still assume that as they grow older, at some point in life they will lose their ability to reason and feel. They have heard stories that the human brain deteriorates because the cells die—as many as a million cells a day—which means that it will soon shrivel up to a lifeless glob.

Not to worry.

First of all, the human brain contains about 100 billion nerve cells (called neurons), all linked by fibers and firing electrical impulses as they transmit information and commands to the rest of the body. Moreover, scientists are now finding that a brain that is kept active may not even be fully grown at age 40. So why can't the human brain be kept healthy and at maximum capacity?

The key word here is *active*, as we will see.

While it is true that in later years large numbers of cells can decline somewhat in effectiveness, much of the chemical messengers and electrical circuitry remain. According to Robert Terry, M.D., Professor of Neurosciences and Pathology at the University of California, San Diego,

> Although the large neurons seem to shrink into the small neuron class, and are thus less able to carry all the brain's functions with quite the efficiency they once had, we now know that these changes are nowhere near as severe as people have suggested in past decades. Given a healthy brain, an intellectually active life and an involvement in society, most people

can remain cognitively effective throughout their lives.

What the good doctor is saying is that the brain can remain vital so long as you challenge it. That's because although not a muscle that must be physically moved, our brain does atrophy if it is not used.

We have said frequently in reference to the body, "Use it or lose it." The same words apply to your brain.

Walter Bortz, M.D., Past President of the American Geriatric Society and Former Co-chairman of the American Medical Association's Committee on Aging, says, "As we allow ourselves to settle into the brain-numbing life pattern that many older people drift down into, senility cannot be far behind."

Two researchers at the National Hospital of Nervous Diseases in London found that the amount of blood reaching the brain decreases by almost 25 percent between the ages of 33 and 61. As the brain receives less oxygen, it can't oxidize as much glucose to produce the electrical energy that operates its functions.

Thus, for those about to retire, there is a double danger when one leaves a mentally stimulating and perhaps physically taxing job for life on the golf course, without having planned activities that will keep his or her brain active.

GUARDING YOUR BODY AGAINST ILLNESS

There is a second and perhaps even more important reason to keep the brain functioning vitally. Psychologist Robert Ornstein and physician David Sobel, in their book *The Healing Brain,* contend that the human brain's main purpose is not only to think but to guard our body from illness. That is, to be an internal health maintenance organization.

But mental exercise alone is not enough. Physical exertion also helps the brain to function better, especially as we get older.

Physical exercise not only increases oxygen intake to clear away fuzzy thinking but it can also chase away feelings of depression and anxiety. The reason it does all this is rather easy to understand. The exerciser's heart pumps more efficiently, sending more oxygen to the brain and boosting the levels of the "good" cholesterol, HDL (high density lipoprotein), which then may reduce certain fat levels.

Research has demonstrated conclusively that exercise and proper diet can provide significant improvement in the level of brain power. The publication, *Perceptual and Motor Skills* (vol. 48, no. 2, 1979), reported on research with a group of people whose average age was 60 and most of whom were afflicted with cardiovascular disease. The subjects were put on a 26-day program of regular exercise and meals high in complex carbohydrates—which provided 80 percent of their daily caloric intake—and low in protein and fats (the Pritikin diet). The result in less than a month was a gain in IQ score and clearer thinking, verbal communication, and intellectual ability.

The investigators noted that this change may have occurred because exercise not only speeds up movement of the body but also increases the speed at which nerve impulses travel between cells.

The measurement of how well a person can extract oxygen from inhaled air and carry it through the body in the bloodstream is called the "VO_2 max." Without exercise, a person's VO_2 max rating generally declines about one percent per year. However, geriatric researchers have estimated that with regular exercise, VO₂ max decline can be reversed by as much as 40 years.

Other researchers have pointed out that exercise is especially important for older persons because such movement helps them retain the *concrete* (or crystallized) intelligence, which one gains through the process of living, while at the same time boosting their *fluid* intelligence, as illustrated in better performance.

Dr. George Sheehan puts it this way: "The fight is never with age but with boredom, with routine, with the danger of not living at all."

Tests have shown that lack of physical activity brings on electrical and chemical changes in the brain wave frequency and, perhaps even more serious, declining levels of two important neurotransmitters: norepinephrine and dopamine, both of which boost the excitement level in the brain. The first of these chemicals, in the form of the hormone adrenalin, is secreted into our systems when we are faced with extreme stress or danger.

Renowned stress expert Dr. Hans Selye has described the process. At the beginning of the stressful time, the pituitary gland secretes the chemical messengers (hormones) ACTH and STH into the bloodstream. These hormones are carried to two small glands above the kidneys (the adrenals) which then produce cortisone and other messengers to prepare the body for "fight or flight." The body goes to "battle stations" by breaking down protein to form sugar for quick energy, thus raising the blood sugar level, driving the blood pressure up, drawing minerals from the bones, and retaining extra salt.

If our intake of nutrients is adequate, we can withstand a great deal of stress and suffer little harm. If it is inadequate, we can become exhausted and vulnerable to disease. That's because the level of transmitters in the brain is influenced by the level of nutrients in the bloodstream. For example, if you take in a large dose of starch, such as a potato, the sudden dose of carbohydrates will tell the brain to produce more serotonin, a chemical that retards brain cell firing and makes us feel relaxed and even sleepy. Most foods have at least a modest effect on mental activity but some are especially strong in "brain food." For instance, substances rich in choline—found in lecithin, egg yolk, fish, cereal, and legumes—increase the chemical ACH, which is thought to lower blood pressure and possibly increase short-term memory.

TWO TYPES OF BRAIN COMMUNICATIONS

The brain, through the central nervous system, sends messages to the body over two "wavelengths." There are the billions of electrical transmissions from neuron to neuron along nerve fibers. Chemical transmitter molecules (called neurotransmitters) are released at some 100 trillion tiny gaps (called synapses) between the ends of the fibers and the next cells. There are also the many glands that release "messengers" (hormones) into the bloodstream to influence our thinking, emotions, and behavior.

Some of those secreted chemicals actually enter the brain to become neurotransmitters. Among them are the endorphins that, when generated by exercise, make one feel good. Marathoners and other athletes refer to this effect as the "runner's high."

The strength and effectiveness of that marvelous group of natural chemicals, and the level of such neurotransmitters, can be enhanced through what we eat as well as from the environment in which we place ourselves. As reported in *Experimental Neurology* (no. 87, 1985), researchers at the University of California, Berkeley, exposed a group of rats to new stimuli, including toys to play with and the company of other rats. The results indicated that age did not prevent the brain from growing. The investigators discovered that even the brains of those creatures who were the equivalent age of a 76-year old human responded and adapted to the new conditions.

More and more scientific research is demonstrating the many links between that flood of nerve impulses and the rest of the body. It is interesting to note that the total electrical power represented by all those neurons is about 20 watts, enough to illuminate a small electric light bulb.

The chemicals manufactured by the brain range from tranquilizers to pain killers to immune system boosters. A number of scientists are now convinced that our emotions, whether they be hope or happiness, joy or dread, or doom and gloom, affect the specific chemicals that the brain manufactures. The thoughts we let pass through our minds might just be transferred into chemical substances in the brain.

Recently, Dr. Candace Pert, Chief of Brain Biochemistry for the National Institute of Mental Health, who discovered the brain's natural opiates, endorphins, and enkephalins, has been involved in research indicating even more links between the nervous system and our immune system; the same chemicals that control our mood are also the key to our physical health.

Perhaps even the expression on your face affects the chemicals produced in your brain. Paul Ekman, Ph.D., psychologist at the University of California, San Francisco, has been quoted as saying, "You become what you put on your face." By this he means that by deciding to change the look on our faces, we may influence the mood in our minds and affect involuntary physiological responses such as heart rate and body temperature.

Among the brain chemicals produced in response to a positive and happy attitude is a hormone from the thymus gland, thymosin-alpha-one. Dr. Nicholas Hall of George Washington University Medical School reported that the level of this "makes-you-feel-good" chemical rose following the subjects' time of ordinary relaxation, as well as after a period of Transcendental Meditation.

Among the natural chemicals, perhaps the most important is the one that "speaks" to the hormone-producing pituitary gland, a small cherry-sized mechanism located at the bottom of the brain just above the roof of your mouth. The pituitary, which has been called the "master gland," produces at least six hormones that influence the body, including our disease-fighting immune system.

And how well our body resists illness is, as we have seen, influenced by our emotions. Research has indicated that people who feel depressed and helpless to control their lives are far more likely to contract a disease than are those individuals who are confident and more or less content with their situations. Among the afflictions that can be affected by emotions, for instance, are heart trouble, diabetes, and Parkinson's disease.

The New York Times Magazine issue of July 28, 1985, in an article entitled "The Stuff of Genius," reported that those environmentally-enriched rats we mentioned earlier developed a greater number of glial cells in their cerebral cortex. These cells, as noted in Chapter Five, seem able to meet the metabolic needs of the neurons, which we now assume are responsible for the brain's mental work. The conclusion from this is that more glial cells in rats given an enriched environment means that the neurons in those creatures were working harder than those in normal rats.

Admittedly, we are assuming that brains in humans function similarly to those in rats, but researchers did find more glial cells in the area of Einstein's brain believed to be concerned with mathematical thinking than in comparable brain areas in a control group. However, these findings may at some point be dismissed because the researchers knew very little about the medical, nutritional, or psychiatric background of the people (former patients in a veteran's hospital) whose brains served as the control group.

Then there was the German scientist Oskar Vogt who, in 1925, following the death of Russian leader V. I. Lenin, took thousands of slides of his brain to study. Vogt announced that there was "marked development of the pyramidal cells" in the cerebral cortex which, the scientist said, produced "an intensification of the general activity of the various divisions of the brain." As reported in the *Journal of the American Medical Association*, Vogt spoke of the large number of paths proceeding from the pyramidal cells that united widely separated parts of the brain. This explains, he declared, the

> wide range and multiplicity of ideas that developed in the brain of Lenin, and particularly his capacity for quickly getting his bearings when confronted with the most complex situations and problems. . . . Lenin's brain activity can be compared, in other words, with a whole wave of sounds closely interwoven, rapidly

tumbling over one another, yet so combined as to produce a mighty harmony.

Mighty harmony indeed. Wouldn't it be wonderful for all humans to encourage brain growth by providing a more stimulating mental (and physical) environment? So, if your life seems to be slowing down, look around for new interests. Get involved in activities that challenge the mind. Studying a new language—which requires memorization and retrieval—is excellent therapy for sluggish neurons. Doing problem-solving exercises or playing word games such as Scrabble are also good brain boosting activities. The best types are those that have you making decisions, then acting on them. Any sort of mental gymnastics that makes the neurons "stretch" rather than "yawn" can increase alertness and keep your brain functioning happily.

Creative pursuits such as painting or sculpting can do the job also. Even reading a good book is a fine way to challenge the cells. On the other hand, watching television is *not,* because this is a passive activity where the mind simply becomes a sponge, absorbing what is on the screen.

Another critical element, according to Doctors Ornstein and Sobel, is positive contact with other people. The brain "draws vital nourishment from our friends, lovers, relatives . . .and even perhaps co-workers and the members of your weekly bowling team."

So, how can you tap the power of your mind? Read on.

USING THE MIND-BODY LINK

For centuries, eastern holy men and philosophers have been telling the world about the "oneness" of the human body-mind-spirit entity. Today, western medicine is beginning to acknowledge this interrelationship and is devising technical specialties that can at least begin to bridge the gap between the mind and the physical body. Such disciplines as behavioral medicine, psychosomatic medicine, and psychotechnologies (which means to help the mind through work on the body) are probing this connection. We know that there is an intricate feedback apparatus that lets the body send messages to the brain on how its actions are doing, allowing self-corrections. This monitoring lets the mind have control over the oxygen level, the body temperature, and the blood chemicals produced.

One problem with this automatic feedback, according to Yale Psychiatry Professor Morton F. Reiser, M.D., in his book *Mind, Brain, Body* (1984), is that in the case of stress or danger, the mind's "alarm bell" continues to keep the body in a state of tension and stress long after the threat that triggered the adrenalin "fight-or-flight" response has gone away.

To counter this, the feedback loop must be interrupted with some sort of "turn-off" process, such as biofeedback and relaxation techniques, meditation, or perhaps taking a walk on the beach or in the woods.

Biofeedback training (BFT), developed in recent years, allows the person to take conscious control of the functions ruled by the brain. Quite simply, biofeedback is a signal from a mechanical device or other outside source indicating what is going on inside you and you respond in a way that makes a change in those internal processes. In short, we can use our willpower to affect how our bodies operate and to change actions over which we may have once thought we had no control. You can choose to change the functions of the autonomic nervous system: body temperature, heart beat, muscle and artery constriction, and so forth.

For example, as author Jackie Dewey points out in her book, *Of Life and Breath* (1987), those with serious asthma problems have achieved up to 80 percent improvement through combining biofeedback training with other techniques. Many patients suffering bronchospasms were able to lower the amount of medication they were taking (some even stopped using it).

Barbara Brown, Ph.D., a pioneer in biofeedback training and author of several books on the subject, points out that much of the success of BFT depends on the contact with the person administering it.

Just as Doctors Ornstein and Sobel have pointed out that in life we draw nourishment from good friendships and close relationships, in the same way, says Dr. Brown, "we're all sensitive to influences like rapport, warmth and understanding . . . [and] equally so to indifference or insensitivity."

So, if someone is learning relaxation to reduce anxiety, for example, a cold, impersonal attitude by the person running the biofeedback machine can be a serious hindrance to success. Biofeedback, like some other "tools" that work because the participant is actively involved and aware of the state of his or her body, is an example of where the patient is no longer the object of the treatment but *is* the treatment. Thus, according to Dr. Brown, "the new authority in healing [and for that matter in health] is the *self*."

Stress reduction, too, can be achieved by conscious effort of the mind. Various meditation techniques have been introduced in the West, designed more or less after the practices of

Indian ascetics but tailored to the western attitude that demands immediate changes. Initially, this situation produced the concept of "instant nirvana" taken up by the drug culture of the 1960s. The problem then, and continuing today, is that a great many of these people missed the point that there is no need to dump or inject foreign substances into the body. As practiced by Tibetan monks and others, the process uses the natural chemicals that exist in all of us.

Meditation techniques first received widespread attention in America in the early 1970s when the Indian Maharishi Mahesh Yogi introduced his Transcendental Meditation. Participants were given a personal mantra, or word sound, to repeat during their twice-daily sessions aimed at stilling the mind.

In succeeding years, many approaches to the "looking inward" process were promoted by various organizations. Also in the 1970s, Harvard Medical School researcher Herbert Benson, M.D., produced specific research describing the physiological changes that occur when the mind becomes quiet, if only for what psychologist Lawrence LeShan called the "Law of the Good Moment."

Dr. Benson, in his best-selling book, *The Relaxation Response*, suggests a simple technique in which a person sits quietly and comfortably, with eyes closed, muscles relaxed as much as possible, and becomes aware of breathing rhythm. The subject then repeats the word "one" slowly and quietly for the duration of the session.

Dr. Nuernberger, in discussing his "Breath Awareness" procedure, suggests that an effective way to focus the mind is to imagine a "very small and still candle flame, or a point of light." Try not to be distracted by the various thoughts that come forth, but concentrate on the flame and your breathing. This technique, he says, will enable you to become more sensitive to the "subtle resource" we call intuition, or "second sight," or even simply a "hunch." "Intuition," he declares, "is the ability to know, without error, beyond the normal boundaries of our reason and intelligence." It is also a powerful tool that can be developed and nurtured, claims Dr. Nuernberger.

In our busy world today, we often ignore the "quiet but clear inner voice that whispers the course we ought to take," long before the intellect "speaks." Getting in touch with intuiting through concentration can open the door to deeper resources of the mind.

Dr. Benson's 1979 book, *The Mind/Body Effect*, stresses that the mind is a more powerful influence on our physical health than we realize, particularly when we are anxious, tense, and under stress. This condition is especially true when our nervous system powers up the "fight-or-flight" response and—unlike our caveman ancestors who sometimes had to tangle with sabertooth tigers—chances are we don't have any surge of physical exercise to release the tension. The result in our "civilized" society is that we end up with long-lasting periods of stress that can be harmful in many ways.

AND HOW ABOUT YOUR OWN PERSONAL BIORHYTHM?

"You need to know when you're hot and when you're not," says environmental physiologist Dr. Carl E. England at the Naval Research Center in San Diego, California. He points out that for most of us, our body systems are governed by an internal clock that is tuned to the pattern of working in daylight and resting in darkness. Heart rate, blood pressure, respiration rate, and body temperature show this, as they go up and down in synchrony with nature's daily rhythm.

What this means is that there are times when mental work can be more effective, when the neurons are more alert with faster chemical activity. Generally, the warmer you feel—unless you have a fever—the more alert you will feel. Dr. England suggests that by keeping an oral thermometer handy and by taking your temperature every waking hour for a week or more you can establish an optimum time to do mental work. Although not always the case, temperatures are often highest in late afternoon, and at low ebb before dawn.

HOW TO USE YOUR MENTAL POWER TO GET THINGS DONE

Realize that before you take an action you probably think, if only for a moment, "If only I could . . ."

The next thought might be to carry the process a bit further, "What if I could . . . ?"

This is often followed by the next step, looking past the desire to think, "If I do that, such and such will happen . . . ."

By now, you are seeing in your mind's eye an image of what you want to do—as if you had accomplished it. You have literally told yourself "I *can* do it" and have pictured what you will have when it is done.

Once you have convinced yourself you *can* do it, there is the "sweet smell of success," but not actual success—yet. Your confidence level has grown. You have seen yourself victorious in your desired change.

Now, retain your picture of success. Let it seep into your subconscious. When you wake up in the morning, bring that image up and look at it. Do this again just before you go to sleep. You are literally programming your mind to make your desire a reality.

As you concentrate on this image, your resolve to do it will grow until it is so powerful that there is nothing left but to go out and do it. Still, to plunge in without considering and drawing upon past experience that can help you is like trying to build a house when you have never done it and are without a set of plans or trained people to help.

You will probably encounter roadblocks and other obstacles in your path. Keep your objective in mind and return again and again to deal with (or to find a way around) those blocks.

Nothing succeeds like persistence. If you believe you need not deteriorate while growing older, you will do things that prevent this from happening. I can safely say this because I am convinced that my positive attitude and refusal to accept what my body was telling me back in 1970 let me get where I am today, in far better physical and mental fitness than I was 20 years ago.

One more caution: Once you have made up your mind what you want to do, don't let yourself, or anyone else, talk you out of it. If you hesitate, or go back and forth, "Should I or should I not do this?" your mind will sense that you are not really convinced you can do it and will offer an easier alternative, "Don't bother, just let things go along as they are."

The way they are? If I had let things go the way they were in 1970 I probably would have died years ago. Or, and this is even scarier, I would be cooped up in a facility for the aged, dying a little each day.

Use your mind to get you started. The more you use it, the more it will work for you.

A good place to start is to say to yourself, "I must get out and move." At first the amount doesn't matter. What does is taking that initial step.

The Confucian philosopher Lao Tzu, in the 6th century B.C., said it best: "The journey of a thousand miles starts with one step."

Well, there you have it. The four self-care areas: your Body—so long as you exercise regularly, Nutrition—including that wonder food Honeybee Pollen, Breathing, and the miraculous Mind. Make a commitment to work on these four areas in your life and I guarantee you will feel better, be better, and look toward the 21st century as I do: with optimism, hope, and an abiding faith that "I am doing the best for my body, mind, and spirit, that I am taking a truly holistic approach to life."

Light workouts with weights is one way Noel stays in condition.

Chapter Eleven

WHAT'S NEXT?

> *Be not afraid of life. Believe that life is worth living and your belief will help create the fact.*
>
> —William James, 1842–1910

I am now in my 90th year of life and plan to continue my exercise and nutrition regimen in order to be able to do the same things at 100 as I do today.

That is, my training program is specifically designed to keep my body and mind in the best possible condition over the next decade.

I truly agree with the host of the PBS televison series *Bodywatch*, Dr. "Red" Duke, who said, "Your body was made for moving" and that, as scientists have suggested, for every hour of physical activity we can gain another hour of life expectancy—or even several more.

EXERCISE AND FITNESS

I plan to run two or three marathon races each year (including the New York Marathon), a schedule which should allow me to see that my physical state is not declining, as it definitely was 20 years ago.

Whatever the weather, Noel takes his road work seriously when training for a marathon.

I also intend to continue boxing because I not only enjoy this sport, but it keeps my eyes and reflexes sharp.

In between these competitive events, I will concentrate on exercises to build up the muscular portion of my legs. Running can do this, but I believe that I can get more pure muscle development during a 15-minute session with weights than by running for an hour.

My overall purpose with this exercise program is to stay in shape to where I am prepared, on short notice, for whatever athletic event people ask me to participate in.

Beyond this, and on my wish list—when I find the time—is skydiving. I'm looking forward to seeing my area of the world from 10,000 feet up, while I float down toward it.

And, again when time permits, I want to be a race car driver. In my mid-20s (as I mentioned in Chapter Two), I promoted one of the first midget car tracks on the West Coast. Now, I want to experience auto racing from the participant's position. If Paul Newman (who is 63) can do it, so can I.

POSITIVE THOUGHT AND NATURAL LAW

Now, you may think all this is a bit ambitious for someone my age. I don't think so. I have already proven, repeatedly, that age need not stop me or anyone else from doing things once thought to be the exclusive domain of "younger" people. I'm convinced that the secret of being able to perform feats you may think are beyond your capability is in the awesome power of the mind. If you truly believe you can do it, then chances are that you can.

However, I also feel that if I can't accomplish what I set out to do, it is because I have neglected something I should have been doing to prepare myself for such challenges. And my preparation is more than mere physical conditioning. I study and read a lot on fitness and—perhaps even more importantly—I listen to my body. That's because, along with a good many other thoughtful people today, I believe that my life—mind and body—is tied in closely with the rhythms of nature.

The ancient Chinese philospher Lao Tzu (discussed in Chapter Nine), believed that nature provides everything without asking payment or thanks, and that strength is found in the Tao, the natural law.

And, Ayurvedic medicine, the 5,000-year old system of natural healing in India that features herbs and exercises (now being adopted by several prominent U.S. physicians), also is based on the premise that to achieve and maintain health one must live in harmony with nature's laws.

That's why, at the end of Chapter Five, I wished you success on "The Path" with "the force of nature."

DANCING

One of those natural rhythms, for me, is ballroom dancing. Some years ago, I went to a local dance academy to learn to "trip the light fantastic." I ended up practicing the tango over and over to where one day the instructor suggested that my partner and I were good enough to dance in competitions.

At the time, I did not see myself traveling around the country displaying my fancy footwork. Now, however, I want to get back to this form of recreation and, who knows, perhaps really take it "on the road."

I enjoy ballroom dancing for two reasons: the pleasure of moving across the floor with a lovely lady in my arms and because the music has always done a great deal for my spirit.

THE "CURRENT" IN MUSIC

As a kid, I played both the baritone saxaphone and the piano. Later, when World War II came along, I discovered the snare drums and joined a local drum and bugle corps. I happily rat-a-tat-tat-ted for the duration of that conflict.

I want to go back to studying the piano; it's my favorite musical instrument. And I'm also itching to take up those drum sticks again. I like that beat; it makes my heart go faster.

But music goes deeper for me than picking out tunes on the ivories or rattling the drums. I'm referring here to the effect of the vibrations we receive from musical sounds and how they resonate in the human body.

Sound, after all, is simply vibrations, and since our whole body is directed by the low-voltage electrical system in the mind and nervous system,[1] sound vibrations can resonate to this

---

[1] Tuning in to the body's electrical system with an outside source of electrical voltage or vibrations is nothing new. It is reported that 2,000 years ago, Roman physicians used the current in electric eels to reduce pain in gout-swollen feet. In recent decades, the healing properties of electrical current have been studied rather extensively. A few years ago, for instance, Andrew Bassett, M.D., Director of the Columbia University—Presbyterian Medical Center's Orthopedic Research Laboratory, developed a device to enhance bone healing by creating a pulsing field of energy (alternating current). That instrument, as well as another method in which electrodes are implanted in the body, has proven to be about 80 percent effective, claims Dr. Bassett.

current. We see this with music, which can affect our emotional state. A march tempo gets us charged up and tapping our feet in time to the beat, while certain types of quiet music relax the mind and allow us to slip into the alpha state of consciousness.

A healing energy is derived from the human voice. Various spiritual movements employ chanting techniques not only as a form of prayer but also as a healing technique. Sitting in a room with a group of people and chanting the same few words over and over may *seem* far removed from western medical practice, but it may not be so alien after all.

In recent years, researchers have discovered that chanting can reduce stress. One experiment involved a group of 32 participants who were to practice relaxation exercises twice daily. Half the group was instructed to perform the exercises in silence. The other half was told to chant a word or phrase during the same exercises. The results demonstrated that those who chanted showed significantly greater chemical changes in their blood of the type that occur during relaxation.

QUIET PURSUITS

For someone who was not exactly an bookworm in school—you will recall that I left the classroom rather early in life—today I do a great deal of reading and often stay up until two or three in the morning immersed in some subject that has caught my interest.

And it seems that my interests are becoming broader by the year. I am constantly looking for books that provide new information about the world around me and lately I have become especially interested in the animal kingdom and how the creatures that share the earth with us live and adapt to life.

Another interest of mine centers on the great variety of human cultures, so I am planning more travel about the world to see how people in other cultures live.

All this study and observation, of course, is excellent exercise for my mind, maintaining a balance with my physical activity.

FOLLOW YOUR STAR

So now you know what is next for me. What about you? What is on your wish list? What have you always wanted to do but were never able to pursue?

Allow me to encourage you to begin challenging yourself, not only in the principal areas of Exercise, Nutrition, Breathing, and Mind Power, but in pursuing any subject that really appeals to you. Broaden your interests, stimulate your mind, and put a new note of excitement in your life.

Why not stop right here and jot down a list of five to ten such projects or activities. Then set up your own personal program to make those dreams come true. Right now think about those dreams. Consider your wishes, whether lifelong or something you thought about as you read this book.

Let me suggest a few ideas to get you started. I'm sure you can come up with many more.

How about a different look at the world around you, such as from a hot-air balloon. In many areas of the United States, particularly in the Southwest where there are large open spaces, professional balloonists will offer rides. They ascend during times of day when the winds are gentle (often early morning or around sunset) and they simply drift along—sometimes quite close to the terrain.

To be even more adventurous, why not combine a trip abroad with a balloon ride as the main event. Two examples are a balloon tour of the French wine country and a balloon safari over the wild game parks in Central Africa. Imagine yourself looking *down* on a herd of giraffes.

If your desires are truly a bit more down to earth, how about a visit to spectacular 620-foot high Bridalveil Falls, in California's Yosemite National Park? Plan to go there in late spring when the falls are running full, while the lodges and campgrounds are not. (Yosemite in October, when the leaves are turning to shades of gold, is also a rare treat.)

Maybe you are fascinated by water in huge, white, frozen, solid masses. You might want to take a cruise on the Inland Passage to Alaska, where your ship can come in quite close to glacial walls higher than a city's tallest buildings. In Canada's Alberta Province, you can drive right up to the Athabaska Glacier and board a tractor-wheeled vehicle for a trip out on the ice.

But let's keep in mind the importance of exercise. Consider a few ideas that can combine your dream with some muscle stretching and healthy breathing.

How about climbing the tallest peak in the "lower 48" states: 14,494-foot Mt. Whitney in California's Sierra Nevada Mountains? The view from the top—not to mention the feeling of accomplishment—is the reward for this. It is a stiff hike, but there is no need for ropes and pitons and no icy expanses to cross. A well-used trail departs from a parking lot on the eastern side of the mountains. Each year, thousands of people take this trail. A popular way to make the climb is to carry a backpack part way up to a camping area, sleep there that night, then walk to the top and all the way back down the next day. You should be in reasonably good condition to attempt it, but if you do you will find many friendly people of all ages along the way.

Would you rather go down than up? Perhaps you have always wanted to see the Grand Canyon from the bottom. You can, of course, stroll down and back (a long and tough walk), but the usual way is to ride a donkey from the rim to the river and return. Through the years, tens of thousands of people have done it, as can you. Be prepared for many hours in the saddle.

Another popular way to enjoy the outdoors and to get good exercise along the way is by paddling a canoe in the Canadian wilderness or in the United States on some of Minnesota's beautiful lakes, for instance. You can go "solo" or join a small group with a guide and all the food and camping equipment provided.

Have you ever thought about bicycling the byways of Europe? It's an inexpensive way to see the countryside and meet the local inhabitants. If you join a bicycle tour group, chances are there will be a vehicle to transport your luggage. All you do is pedal, at an easy pace, from one village to the next. Often, you will find yourself staying either in local inns or perhaps at an inexpensive hostel, where you are likely to meet people from many countries.

If the people you're looking forward to meeting are distant family members, and you want them to come to you, maybe your fantasy has been to locate all your living relatives and have one giant gathering. This could be a mentally and physically challenging task, with detective work to find the people (you may even have to construct a good part of the family tree), then staging the reunion. Actually, you will probably want help from a "task force" of close relatives. You develop the plans and decide how they are to be carried out. You are in charge and you are the guiding force to see that it comes to pass.

On the other hand, if you really want to see some distant and exotic places, and perhaps have always wanted to wade ashore on some remote island in the South Pacific, consider cruises that specialize in such things. Best known is Salen Lindblad Cruising, whose journeys often involve shore visits accomplished in a Zodiac rubber boat. Among cruise destinations are the Galapagos Islands, the Spice Islands of Indonesia, and remote outcroppings in the Indian Ocean.

Society Expeditions, headquartered in Seattle, has cruises that let passengers experience the natural history, wildlife, and primitive cultures in remote corners of the globe ranging from Antarctica and the Northwest Passage to Mauritania, New Guinea, or Senegal.

In a somewhat tamer approach, Exploration Cruises' small but comfortable ships often go right up on a tropical beach, allowing passengers to walk ashore without getting their feet wet.

These are just a few possibilities. What are your dream-of-a-lifetime ideas? And, don't fear to be a bit outrageous. Let your imagination run free.

Now, if your imagination seems just to sit there saying, "Huh?" maybe it's because you have not used your mind much in recent years. Those brain cells might be a little sluggish. Mine certainly were when I decided at age 70 to take control of my life and to think for myself.

It was not an easy task, as for some years I had been a person who waited to see what tomorrow would bring. My attitude back then was "I can't do anything about it, so I'll just have to go along with whatever happens." Talk about giving away control of my life! As I have said, my doctor warned me that I probably would not survive any activity that would require exertion. My miserable state was dragging me down the steep path toward an early demise.

Fortunately, once I began making my own decisions, I found—as scientists are now proving—that even the long underused mind can come back to life and begin working again.

Once that magnificent part of our anatomy is functioning properly, there is virtually no limit to what it can do, and it is on the job 24 hours a day. For example, new ideas just seem to pop into my mind when I'm least expecting them. Now, I sometimes wake up in the middle of the night with the answer to things I have been thinking about.

I am fully convinced that it was my mind that provided the power for me to become who I am today.

My wish is that you tap into that same power. With it, you will not be afraid of trying new ideas and activities. Most of all, it will serve you rather than you serving it.

At that point, your answer to the question, "What's next?" can be a whole new and exciting approach to living.

HAVING TROUBLE GETTING MOTIVATED?

A sad fact is that even today, when so many people are aware of the emphasis on being fit from communities, government agencies, and the media, only about 20 percent of adult

Americans regularly do the amount of activity recommended to provide cardiovascular and respiratory fitness.

The President's Council on Physical Fitness and Sports lists six old (but still widely used) excuses about exercise:

- I'm too busy, I don't have time.
- Working out is so inconvenient.
- Working out hurts my bad knee.
- Exercise cuts into my family time.
- Exercise is boring.
- Exercise has to hurt to provide results.

The truth is, none of these should be drawbacks to regular fitness training, for there are responses to all these excuses.

In a recent article in *Prevention Magazine* entitled, "Ten Ways to Stay Motivated," writer Tom Shealey outlined ideas to allow anybody to keep up a program of regular walking:

- Get the Big Mo (momentum) that professional athletes use by pacing yourself up ahead of each session.
- Read up on walking and learn how much variety there is.
- Pretend you're walking across the country.
- Add variety to your walking regimen.
- Set goals.
- Walk with someone.

- Remember all the calories you will burn.
- Walking keeps you warm in cold weather.
- Plan a walking vacation for spring or summer.
- Join a walking club.

These are good ideas, no matter which particular form of exercise you choose for your fitness program.

Noel with his 9 great grandchildren. Back row from the left: Justin, Mitchell, Noel, Micah, Lily Noelle, and Jason. Front row: Joseph, Jeremy, Benjamin, and John.

Chapter Twelve

THE CARE-FOR-YOURSELF PROGRAM

"Good Morning World. Here I Am!
—Noel Johnson, 1899–

INTRODUCTION

Several years ago, I met a 90-year old Russian scientist, A. R. Kaminsky. He was traveling about the world collecting and analyzing various types of bee pollen for their nutrient content. One day, he remarked to me, "When you reach our age, if you are not doing something for someone else, what good are you doing for yourself?"

In the early pages of this book, I have described what I did for myself by turning my life around. Then, in subsequent chapters, we looked at the four basic keys to my health today: Exercise, Nutrition, proper Breathing, and Mind Power. Now, I want to do something for you, the reader.

So this chapter contains specific steps that will put you "on the path." First, however, let me stress the point that the ultimate responsibility for our health and well-being lies within ourselves. Thus, in order to regain lost health, each person must construct his or her own self-care program. And, such a program could require drastic changes in life-style. Mine did.

Still, if you adopt a program that incorporates the four areas discussed here, and follow it faithfully for at least 100 days, I am confident that not only will you feel better—perhaps better than you have ever felt—but you will find yourself looking toward continuing it as you see your life being transformed.

Before we begin, let me make two comments. This program is designed to complement—not replace—conventional medical techniques and treatments where they are needed in the event of illness or injury. However, in my own experience I find I have far less need to contact my doctor than I did before I finally took charge of my life 20 years ago.

In addition, far too many people today are looking for instant solutions to their problems. Books and magazine articles are filled with promises that seem to be an easy answer. In most cases, however, the body's decline into premature aging and disease was the product of years of neglect; to reverse the process will take time and effort also. Thus, any worthwhile self-care program to counter aging and deterioration must include a firm and long-term commitment to stay with it.

Now to my four-level blueprint for health and life.

Mind Power

True and long-lasting individual change comes not from being told by others what to do, but from the dictates of one's conscience, guided by personal values and beliefs. Certainly, the most overriding factor in living healthy to 100 and beyond is your mental attitude. Without control of your mind, chances for success with the other elements are slim. "We have thought ourselves into what we are," says veteran actor, broadcaster and motivation specialist Bob Collier, adding that mental attitude "is the result of the current of one's thoughts, ideas, feelings and beliefs."

Mr. Collier addresses quite a few areas to mobilize in a quest for health. That's why our goal here is to alter our belief in ourselves and what we can do. We must regain control over our bodies and treat them in a way that allows them to rebuild themselves and bring us back to health. To do this, we must reprogram our biological computer—the mind.

Let's consider some reprogramming strategies.

1. When you wake up in the morning, do as I do. Just as you open your eyes, smile, and say out loud (or quietly), "Good morning world, here I am." Spoken with feeling, this sentence plants a positive affirmation in the subconscious mind, and we begin the day on an optimistic note.

2. Lie quietly for a few minutes, take a few deep breaths and tell yourself what you want to accomplish today.

3. Give first priority to those things you have already started, but be willing to take on new tasks with enthusiasm.

4. Don't accept at face value the popular notion that "thoughts are things." Instead, consider that thoughts do not become things until you put those thoughts into action.

5. When you get up, begin by *not* doing exactly what you did the day before. If you always put a sock on your right foot first, today start with the left one. If you habitually head for the coffeemaker for that wake-up cup, this time pour a glass of fruit juice instead and *then* brew the coffee. In other words, try not to let your life become too routine. By varying your actions, you force your mind to be aware of the changes so that it must work a bit more.

6. As you progress through your day, don't let yourself become upset or bogged down about things over which you have no power. Remember St. Francis of Assisi's prayer: "Oh God, grant me the serenity to accept the things I cannot change, the courage to change the things I can, and the wisdom to know the difference between ."

7. Keep in mind that, really, only you are responsible for your life. Don't delegate this authority away, as I almost did, to a well-meaning relative or friend.

8. Set aside 10 to 15 minutes of "quiet time" each day, where you can sit either in formal meditation or simply alone with your thoughts.

9. At the end of the day, as you prepare for bed, let yourself think briefly about what you need to do tomorrow and what your priorities are. Then, as you settle down to sleep, let your mind drift gently away from tasks by telling yourself "I've done all I can do today and it is OK to rest now." Concentrate on "seeing" in your mind's eye a pleasant image or scene

that you can thoroughly enjoy. I suggest envisioning a beautiful mountain meadow in the sunshine, the seashore with the continuous roll of the waves, or a peaceful setting that is special to you.

Exercise

1. Choose an effective aerobic exercise such as walking, bicycling, running, swimming, low-impact aerobic dancing, exercycle (stationary bicycle), or hiking.
2. Set up a firm schedule for yourself, allotting at least two times a week to do this exercice.
3. Try to avoid scheduling your exercise right after you get up, before your body is warmed up. I recommend late afternoon or early evening. (Don't forget to do some warm-up stretches first.) By then, you give your heart and lungs a workout and reduce stress levels from the work day. Exercising just before dinner will reduce your appetite because appetite-suppressing adrenalin will be released in your bloodstream. As a bonus, you will probably sleep better on exercise days.
4. Begin your exercise program slowly, and gradually increase the level of intensity. You should not be exhausted at the end of 20 minutes. If you begin to feel pain while exercising, slow down or stop for a while. Over-training can lead not only to more pain but to damage that may force you to stop your program for several weeks.

5. If you find yourself becoming bored with the exercise you have chosen, look for a second (or even third) way to get your workout, then alternate the exercise sessions. Or arrange to exercise with a friend; time flies when you are also enjoying a conversation or just being with someone else.

6. Following the evening meal, go for a relaxed walk so that your digestive system can do its work comfortably while you are upright and your body organs are being moved gently.

7. Keep a written record of your progress, noting the date of each outing, how long you exercised (not how far you went, as the time is more important than distance), and some indication of the intensity. For instance, "Today, when I reached my full pace, I found I was walking at a speed of three steps per second."

8. Or, count your pulse rate as you walk. You will need a stop watch or one with a sweep second hand. Count the pulse beats for 10 seconds, then multiply by six, and you have your rate per minute. For greatest efficiency, your heart rate should be between 70 and 85 percent of its maximum level. To find out how you are doing, subtract your age from 220 and multiply that number by 75 percent. Then compare your heart rate with the result. For example, if you count 20 pulse beats during those 10 seconds, your heart is pumping at 120 beats per minute. If you are 60 years old, your maximum heart is 220 minus 60, or 160 beats per minute. Since your actual heart rate of 120

is 75 percent of 160, you are working your heart at 75 percent of its capacity.

Most important is that the exercise should be one you enjoy, one that does not involve extensive skill or a particular technique that must be learned (unless, of course, you already have this skill or technique), one that does not promote injury, and one that you can do alone, if necessary. It should also be one that does not require extensive equipment (such as the muscle-working machines in health clubs and fitness centers), but one that allows you to take your exercise when and where you choose.

If you say, "The exercise I prefer is walking to the refrigerator during television commercials," score yourself a minus 10 and go back to square one. Your exercise must get your heart rate up, your muscles moving, and your blood flowing more vigorously as you bring in more oxygen by breathing more deeply.

Nutrition

Your body needs at least 40 different nutrients for optimum health. Because most foods contain a number of these, you are better able to obtain at least some of the needed nutrients by varying the types of food you consume from day to day.

1. Remember that as we get older our bodies require fewer calories, so curtailing intake while continuing to exercise can prevent weight gain, which as we have previously noted is a key element in several diseases.

2. It is equally important to make sure you receive all the vitamins and minerals your body needs. For many people, an excellent way to insure a steady flow of

many nutrients is to take some fresh honeybee pollen on a daily basis.

3. Since it is usually difficult to simply stop eating certain foods our body has craved for many years, I recommend that people simply eat less of them. The "grazing concept" mentioned in Chapter Seven really works for humans.

Breathing

1. Stand tall. It is all too easy, when you are feeling tired or depressed, to walk about with slumped shoulders and head bent forward. When you straighten up, you breathe more air into your lungs with less effort. Your heart, in turn, receives more power to function. Standing tall allows you to look at yourself in the mirror and say, "I'm an individual, a special person. I am somebody." In short, you have given yourself a positive affirmation. In addition, by keeping your back straight (but not rigid) you put less pull on your spine and your organs function better because they are operating in the space alloted them.

2. Breathe from the diaphragm so that the lungs can operate efficiently and at maximum capacity.

3. Breathe through your mouth part of the time, especially when exercising, in order to breathe more deeply.

4. Try pursed lip breathing, especially if you suffer from impaired breathing caused by asthma, bronchitis, or

emphysema. Breathing through barely open lips allows you to draw more power from your lungs.

So there you have them, the elements needed for a personal self-care program. The principal ingredient, however, involves interpretting self-care to mean *care for yourself*, for that concern is the fuel that can power you to be healthy to 100 and beyond.

May these words be helpful in your quest: "Make an endless wish. If you concentrate and perfect yourself, you will break through the barriers."[1]

---

[1] From a "prayer" recited by a Japanese gymnast as he entered the finals competition at the 1984 Olympic games, Los Angeles, and won the Gold Medal.

Chapter 13

THE CHIROPRACTIC CONNECTION

The entire thrust of this book is to project the importance of exciting and vital health!

Chiropractic Assistant Bari Evans and Noel Johnson

153

I sincerely feel that we must turn our thoughts away from illness and disease. Thinking must be elevated to thoughts of happiness and health. Vitality, strength, and longevity will certainly follow this line of reasoning.

Responsibility

Nutrition to the human body is akin to gasoline and oil to the automobile. If people continue to use inferior products in their vehicles, the cars will not run properly and will be assured of repeated break-downs and financial burdens to the owners. The vehicles will have an early demise when excessive speed, jack-rabbit starts, slamming on the brakes repeatedly, and other forms of reckless actions continue.

If, however, people respect and care for their automobiles, i.e. check the working parts frequently, add quality fuels, lubricate the chassis at proper intervals, and keep the interior and exterior clean, the cars will last far beyond their expected life span.

Comparison

Though similar preventative steps are necessary in the human body, to maintain health and prevent disease, the stated correlation seems to end there, because we are talking about inanimate objects and animate subjects. When a part wears out in a car, it is merely a matter of simple replacement. If a portion of the human body anatomy is diseased or destroyed – though science has developed and perfected some duplicate parts that work – there is always the potential danger in even a simple type of operation or procedure. This is why we must love, give attention to, and diligently care for our most magnificent possession...our body.

The thoughts expressed above gravitated my thinking to the chiropractic profession...

In 1895, four years before I was born, Dr. D.D. Palmer of Davenport, Iowa, gave his first spinal adjustment and brought hearing back to a man named Harvey Lillard, who had been deaf for seventeen years. That correction was the beginning of the great profession known as chiropractic. Like most people, I heard about chiropractic years ago. Relatives and friends told me of the various appointments they made to their chiropractor, and I was amazed at all the different health problems that seemed to be corrected by spinal care. Not only were people with backaches helped, but headaches, respiratory problems, digestive disorders, shoulder distress, and a host of other conditions related to the nervous system.

A skeptical outlook

My first introduction to chiropractic resulted because of an injury sustained while working in the back yard of my home. I had been digging in the garden and wrenched my lower back while moving a loaded wheel-barrow. I immediately went to bed and later that afternoon my son visited me and suggested that I visit a chiropractor. Even though I was in pain I was apprehensive and listened to scare tactics by some, (I believed at that time), authorities. Therefore, I refused his suggestion.

I was in bed for about 3 weeks and my condition continued to deteriorate. It was possible for me to lie in bed but the minute I attempted to stand on my feet, the stabbing pain returned.

Decision

While lying in bed, I read various papers and magazines and one time browsed through a quotation encyclopedia. I read several pages and one paragraph seemed to jump right out at me. It was a quotation by Spencer, wherein he stated: "There is a principle which is a bar against all information, which is proof against all argument, and which cannot fail to keep a man in everlasting ignorance. That principle is condemnation before investigation."
I almost felt the quotation was written especially for me. Right then I decided to read everything I could get my hands on about chiropractic.

The Triangle of Health

The chiropractic belief that total health is represented by a geometric triangle was understandable to me, i.e. the base plane structural (balance), one of the angled planes chemical (nutritional), and the other mental (emotional). As long as the three sides are in harmony, there will be health. If there is a distortion of any of the three qualities, there will no longer be symmetry, therefore, the amount of loss of health depends upon the severity of distortion. Simply, you cannot change one of these factors without effecting the other two. Further, chiropractors base their major concept on the structural factor of the body. Even in normal living there is always slight stress of gravity pull plus the weight of the individual that has to be accommodated for continually. Any increase beyond this normal stress will effect the structure of the body and thereby the nervous system.

The name chiropractic...

Chiropractic was named by Dr. Samuel H. Weed, a minister well versed in ancient languages. Chiropractic is a word composed from the Greek; 'cheir' meaning the hand, and 'praktos' meaning done; hence, done by hand.

The chiropractic forte...

The communication system in the body is activated, perpetuated, and controlled by the nervous system. The brain initiates nerve impulses which pass through the spinal cord, then out via the spinal nerves, to a nerve communicating network which supplies all the tissues and organs of the body. There is a return route back to the brain following the reverse steps mentioned.

The area of greatest danger or pressure upon transmission of nerve impulses is in the spinal column region.

Chiropractors have found that potential injury to this area is rather common because of the necessity of the human being to be mobile, and though nature has housed the spinal cord in a most protective casing, it is susceptible to stress and injury at any given time, by external forces or internal weakness.

My initial experience...

I consider myself to be a very logical person and as I stated earlier, my injured condition was not improving, in fact the pain was actually becoming a part of me. After I read the material about chiropractic, i.e. what it is, what it does, and what a patient can expect from its treatment, I decided to visit a local chiropractor.

Dr. Rudy Fahlbusch, a graduate of two excellent chiropractic colleges in this country, a past member and president of the California State Board of Chiropractic Examiners, met me at the door and escorted me into the examining room. Then took x-rays of my spine and showed me the area of distress. The misalignment problem was very obvious. I was placed on a chiropractic table and the doctor proceeded to align my spinal column. When the vertebrae were returned to their proper position, I felt a slight 'click' or 'snap' and almost immediately recognized some relief in the injured area. The adjustments (as they call them) were painless, and not the horrendous pain that I had always visualized. I returned home and went to bed to rest and returned to the office for further correction the following day. After two weeks, I was out running once again. I attend the chiropractic office on a fairly consistent schedule because I always strive to be in the greatest physical condition, and know that this type of care is essential for my very best performance. I am acquainted with a great many athletes, throughout the country, that feel the same way as I do about chiropractic care.

Study requirements...

The average chiropractor is well qualified by educational standards. After graduating from high school, there is a mandatory two-year pre-chiropractic study curriculum required prior to being accepted in a chiropractic college. When the doctorate is achieved, four-years later, it is then necessary to pass a state board examination to qualify the doctor the right to be licensed in the state. After that six-year study period, the doctor must attend a seminar once a year to qualify for the license renewal rights.

Babies, Children, Adults and Senior Citizens...

If I had the power to direct mankind, I would make sure that all people understand the fantastic value of chiropractic. This world of ours will be a much happier and healthier place if we rid stress from our lives. With all the problems in the world today, I feel that chiropractic is a valuable answer to many health conditions, it is the largest drugless profession, and regardless of age, it is my belief that everyone will benefit from this marvelous type of care.

The most advanced computer in the world is prehistoric in comparison to the marvelous capabilities of the human mind and body. When the body is healthy it is akin to beautiful music being played by a very fine instrument, and the virtuoso assuring the greatest rhythm of the body is a competent chiropractor. One must also remember that the body is not a solid structure. The greatest athletes and dancers know that the strength of grace and rhythm of motion, of any person, depends upon optimum synchronization of total body function. This is the reason that I, again, stress the great importance of regular visitation dates to your chiropractor. The major importance of spinal care is to prevent problems before they become a health factor. Live a healthy and happy life.

Noel Johnson preparing for his 7th New York City Marathon Race Nov. 5, 1989. He began at 80 and is now 90 years of age.

Chapter 14

THE MOST HUMAN INSTINCT IS TO SURVIVE

Throughout this past century we have had many people in various occupations tell us what we should do to have health and longevity. No one, however, as of today has given us the formula for living so that we may escape any or all of the epidemics that destroy millions and millions of people of all races. There consistently seems to be new diseases that increase this toll of death.

The marvelous body our creator gave us at the birth of Mankind is in desperate straits. Sadly, there doesn't appear to be one person in the world that has the wisdom to know the reason for this calamity, nor the power to stop its dangerous progression.

Think of it...Why do we become sick before we die? Is it not logical to believe that without sickness we would not die? If this is true, the only reason we become sick is because of our life style. We work against the laws of nature, and it is essential that these laws be obeyed. Also, we must realize that man cannot create food that has all the nutrients the body requires to rebuild itself and continue its health.

Sickness creates terrific profits for some specialized groups. More income than any other industry in the world. Is this the reason the trend continues and increases, year after year? The only purpose for not accomplishing a 'disease-free America' surely must be for the sake of garnering this enormous financial windfall. I always believed that any goal in life can be reached, good or bad, depending upon the dedication of proper or improper methods.

Life was never meant to be easy.

The medical people should know and inform the public what causes certain health conditions, but this facet is not taught in their schooling, so you cannot expect them to do this. Look around and think! Who is there to warn the public? I believe we should have a new governmental department formed, but where are the individuals that have the wisdom to do this? There is a health department in existence now, but I don't believe nine out of ten people questioned would be able to tell you what they are doing.

This discussion must bring realization, of the problem we face, back to each concerned individual. We desperately need a self care program. I am sure we can each take care of our individual selves better than anyone else has done in our past history, and the profit incentive would be ours. This self help procedure is active in many countries of the world. I have learned a great deal about this matter during my travels, and have experienced a personal attitude change on this whole subject.

We, too, are responsible...Don't forget your actions in the past have created your present condition, and if you want an improvement it will take dedicated work, but I'm sure you can accomplish the goal you seek. The reason we have health or sickness is controlled by each of us. We created our own destiny by the power of our mind, and we can be what we want to be.

Your body cures itself if it operates without deficiencies.

To make a change in our physical and mental conditions we must first make a change in our life styles. We have to pay attention to this fact every day. We do not necessarily have to change the type of food we eat, but we must change the amount of what we eat. The quantity is most important. We get addicted and crave what we have been eating for years, although much of the intake is destructive to our wellbeing. There is usually good nutrients in most everything eaten, however, do not eat too much at one time, so your digestive, eliminating, organs can dispose of the waste easily, and not have the excess be placed in storage for future use – it will tend to make you overweight and in time the fat will putrify, then you will begin to give off body odors. This is the primary reason for the offensiveness of some people. Very few of us really require the amount of food we eat. I often wonder why so many people over eat and then go on a diet? It is said that, "When your stomach becomes larger than your chest, get your box ready."
If you eat three square meals a day, as so many advise, you will be in the hospital soon. This could be very true because everyone likes to eat and the hospitals are full.

"I'm glad I'm 90 years young – not 65 years old" Noelism.

Why do we get old, and it seems our body begins to degenerate after just a few years of living? The reason is because we have a deficiency of some nutrient that the body needs. It rebuilds itself continually, and we begin accomodating to that deficiency.

It sounds strange, but we are not all there. Why? Because there is no man made food that possesses all the nutrients the body requires to nourish, sustain, and build itself completely. Therefore, as the years go by the deficiency increases – and the greater it becomes the less control we have over our body. How far could you get with your automobile if you didn't replenish it with gas? How many years can we live if we do not furnish our bodies with the proper nutrients?

At the age of 90 I claimed, "I Found The Fountain of Youth," I was talking about the nutrient that has all the body requirements to rebuild itself without a deficiency. Honey bee pollen was gifted for mankind at the time of creation – it is not man made. it is the miracle food of the world today, as it was at the time of creation. This food has rebuilt my body.
Pollen is a necessity for longevity. It is one of the purest foods discovered by man. Its grains contain the male germ cells from the flowering plants for fertilization of other plants. Pollen is needed for all vegetation. It has life that no man made food can possibly produce. This is the food that humans need to complete their nutritional necessities, so there will be no deficiencies.
The amazing powers of this gift from the bees has been known all over Europe and Russia for centuries. In my travels to Asia, I found that Orientals also used bee pollen as a cherished health food.
"Honey bee pollen is the world's most perfect food." This fact can hardly be disputed since pollen has been analyzed and its ingredients proven in laboratories around the entire world. Fresh honey bee pollen is the only food that contains all the essential nutrients necessary to sustain life. What

more can be said, it has done remarkable things for me and I know it will as long as I continue its use. Like other foods, some pollen is much better than others – due to the way it is produced for the market.

"*Get the best you can and you will be better than you have ever been*" Noelism.

IN CONCLUSION: A CHALLENGE

At the beginning of this book, I spoke of a promise, the promise that we do not have to be sick, that we can prevent illness and even turn our lives around from severe debility. I have related how I transformed myself from a sickly old man to a healthy, active middle-ager turning 90.

We will soon enter the 21st century, an exciting transition now little more than a decade away. During the remaining years in this century, you can change your life and be able to enter the new century perhaps in far better physical and mental condition than you now enjoy.

That is why I now issue this challenge to you, the reader: Take charge of your life today and start working toward living healthy to 100 and beyond!

If you are healthy as you read this, look upon a personal self-care program as an "insurance policy" to protect your health and well-being in the years to come. If, on the other hand, you are beginning to feel a bit like the sickly creature I once was, use my challenge as your motivation to start turning life around.

In either case, recognize that the process will take time. Chances are it took years to degenerate into ill health. Give yourself time to return to good health.

Don't be like most people who start out with good intentions to institute an exercise program, only to quit in a few weeks or months.

Look upon your commitment as a life-long process to achieve long-life results.

Realize that being healthy is worth effort and that health is within your grasp.

As Dr. Lenore Zohman observed in 1981, following the comprehensive physical evaluation I underwent just before running my second New York Marathon,

> As more and more people engage in regular activity into old age, it becomes clearer that advanced age can be a time of dynamic health. . . . Thus regular exercise may help add a few years to our lives. But perhaps more important is the potential that exercise has for adding joy, vitality and "life" to our years, as exemplified by Noel Johnson.

It is clear to me that my recovery of health is due to making changes in my life-style to live in accord with natural laws. Nature counsels moderation in food and drink, movement (remember the grazing animals), proper breathing, and a healthy mental attitude. When we choose to ignore this counsel, the result often is stress and distress, followed by sickness.

Fortunately, there are indications that more and more of us are paying attention to this advice.

The Trend Analysis Program of the American Council of Life Insurance listed three possible futures for the next half-century of health care:

1. An emphasis on the routine use of high technology,

2. Increasing governmental responsibility, and
3. Individual responsibility and "wellness."

The third option was described in a report from an imaginary commission of the Program, as if looking back from the year 2030. It noted that "Two basic premises had emerged by the end of the 20th century: that medicine had little or nothing to do with health and that there were few limits to an individual's responsibilities for his or her health."

The imaginary report went on to note that, "By the early 1990's most people accepted the body as its own finest laboratory. Children were taught techniques that allowed the body to adapt naturally and overcome illnesses."

Fantasy, you say? Read on.

"It's never too late to get fit." Under that headline, a University of California, Berkeley, *Wellness Letter* stated, "Over 50 doesn't mean over the hill, even for people who have never exercised regularly. Despite years of sedentary living, it is still possible to become physically fit...." In a study of three groups of men between the ages 45 and 55, Dr. Kash, Director of the Exercise Physiology Laboratory at San Diego State University, found that men who had never exercised before could achieve levels of fitness almost equal to those of their counterparts who had exercised regulary for 10 years. One formerly sedentary group actually reversed the aging process and raised its average maximum heart rate during the course of the study, (periods of 6, 7, or 10 years). These men were, in the crucial terms of aerobic capacity, younger at the end of the program than they had been at the beginning.

Finally, listen to Nobel Laureate Alexis Carrel, writing in 1935, in his highly acclaimed book *Man the Unknown:*

For the first time in history, humanity, helped by science, has become master of its destiny. . .[but] to progress again, man must remake himself. . . .We cannot undertake the restoration of ourselves. . . before having transformed our habits of thought. . . . There are, as we know, two kinds of health, natural and artificial. Scientific medicine has given to man artificial health and protection against most infectious diseases. It is a marvelous gift. But man is not content with health that is only lack of malady and depends on [among other things] periodical medical examinations and the expensive attention of hospitals, doctors and nurses. . . . He wants natural health, which comes from resistance to infectious and degenerative diseases, from equilibrium of the nervous system. He must be constructed so as to live without thinking about his health.

That's what we have been talking about, *natural health, living within nature's laws to 100 and beyond.*

Be well.

Now at 90: The Fountain of Youth

Ever since Ponce de León sailed the oceans searching for the Fountain of Youth, each generation has wondered where it is and how to contain it. Throughout my life of 90 years, I have heard about this fountain and wondered why it was so mysterious.

At age 70, when I was at my all-time low, I started to rebuild my body by changing my way of living. At 80, even though I had made great improvements, I did not claim that I had found the Fountain of Youth, because I was in the physical condition I was supposed to be in for a person of my age who had been living right all along. But I began to realize how few people were in the physical condition I was. This, I thought, must be because I was doing something that my body needed. Many people were older than 80, but none had the physical condition I had.

I know that one of the nutrients that I have been taking for the past 12 years—the fresh High Desert Bee Pollen—gives me the nutrients I need so that there is no deficiency of any kind in my body. Deficiencies are what cause us to degenerate and to become old. As with anything worth having, life with health is not meant to be easy. To succeed we must exert an effort and be deserving of what we want. High Desert Bee Pollen meets my body's needs and enables me to keep it at maximum potential. It fills the gaps and I do the work.

Now at 90, I will soon be living in my third century. Now at 90, I look younger, I am told, and I am in better physical and mental condition than I was at age 70. Now at 90, I am *entitled* to claim that I have found the Fountain of Youth. Unlike others who make the same assertion, I have more than just longevity upon which to base my claim. I have the vigor and vitality now at 90 that only young people are supposed to have. Truly, I have found the Fountain of Youth.

—*Noel Johnson*